MOREH NEVUCHIM

מורה נבוכים

טעמי המצות

Part III
Chapters 26-54

The Mitzvos
Including Comments from Ramban

Translated and Annotated by
Rabbi Avraham Yaakov Finkel

YESHIVATH BETH MOSHE
SCRANTON, PA.

Yeshivath Beth Moshe
930 Hickory Street, Scranton, PA 18505
(570) 346-1747

First Edition

Contents

הקדמה
מראש הישיבה
מורינו הרב יעקב שניידמאן שליט״א

הרמב״ם פתח ספרו משנה תורה בהל׳ דעות. ולדעתי נראה פשוט דטעמו דההקדמה ללימוד תורה הוא דעות ישרות עפ״י תורה, ומי שאין דעותיו ישרות ומכוונות לפי המסורה אף לימודו יהיה להבל וריק, ולא עוד אלא שלימודו יסייע אותו לילך לתרבות רעה. ומהתורה גופא יביא ראיות לדעותיו הכוזבות ולסתור אמונת הי״ת. חז״ל אמרו דאלישע בן אבויה (שידוע לנו בשם אחר) יצא לתרבות רעה משום דמתחלה לא מסרו אביו ללימוד התורה אלא משום שראה כבוד שיש לתלמדי חכמים והיה תחלתו שלא לשמה, ומזה יצא לתרבות רעה עד שאמר בירושלמי דבשעה שעמד מבית המדרש היה נופל ממנו ספרי אפיקורסות של היוונים. וכן בדורינו ראינו שאם אין יסודות האמונה והבטחון ודרך הלימוד הכל עפ״י המסורה מדורות ראשונים, יש סכנה עצומה. וזהו גם טעמו בהקדמותיו הנפלאות למשנה תורה ולפירושו על משניות להעמיד יסודות באמונה ובדרך הלימוד. ועוד חיבר ספרו מורה נבוכים שבתוכו יש יסודות חזקות באמונה ובאיזה דרך להבין התורה.

והנה ידוע דיש מקומות בספרו מ״נ שפירש ענינים שלדעתנו הם זרים ואינם לפי המסורה שלנו. וא׳ מהם הוא ביאורו בטעם הקרבנות. ועיין רמב״ן ויקרא פר׳ א׳ פסוק ט׳ וז״ל והנה בכתוב הזה טעם הקרבנות שהם אשה ריח ניחוח לה׳. ואמר הרב במורה הנבוכים (ג מו) כי טעם הקרבנות, בעבור שהמצרים והכשדים, אשר היו ישראל גרים ותושבים בארצם מעולם, היו עובדים לבקר ולצאן, כי המצרים עובדים לטלה והכשדים עובדים לשדים אשר יראו להם בדמות שעירים, ואנשי הודו עד היום לא ישחטו בקר לעולם. בעבור כן צוה לשחוט אלה השלשה מינין לשם הנכבד כדי שיודע כי הדבר שהיו חושבים כי הם בתכלית העבירה הוא אשר יקריבו לבורא, ובו יתכפרו העונות. כי כן יתרפאו האמונות הרעות שהם מדוי הנפש, כי כל מדוה

וכל חולי לא יתרפא כי אם בהפכו. אלה דבריו ובהם האריך והנה הם דברי הבאי, ירפאו שבר גדול וקושיא רבה על נקלה, יעשו שולחן ה׳ מגואל שאיננו רק להוציא מלבן של רשעים וטפשי עולם, והכתוב אמר כי הם לחם אשה לריח ניחוח עכ״ל. ופשוט דלא היה כוונת הרמב״ם שזה סוף הטעם של מצות קרבנות, והוא בעצמו כתב ביד בהל׳ מעילה פ׳ ח׳ הל׳ ח׳ וז״ל וכל הקרבנות כולן מכלל החוקים הן, אמרו חכמים שבשביל עבודת הקרבנות העולם עומד, שבעשיית החוקים והמשפטים זוכין הישרים לחיי העולם הבא, והקדימה תורה ציווי על החוקים, שנאמר ושמרתם את חקותי ואת משפטי אשר יעשה אותם האדם וחי בהם עכ״ל. ומבואר בדעתו שיש טעמים כמוסים ונכבדים לעבודת הקרבנות. אולם הרי הראשונים שנתנו טעם למצוות לא היה כוונתם שזה סוף טעם המצוה שבודאי יש טעמים אחרים רק רצו לתת טעם כדי לחזק קיום המצוה אצל ההמון ועוד דהטעם שנתנו הוא אמת והוי בכלל לימוד תורה. ובביאור המחלוקת נראה דאף הרמב״ן ידע דלא היה כוונת הרמב״ם לומר שזה סוף טעם מצות קרבנות ומ״מ תפש עליו משום דלדעתו לא הוי טעם כלל ואינו אמת, שאין לומר שכל עבודת הקרבנות הוא רק שלא נכשל בטעות עובדי ע״ז וע״ז חולק הרמב״ם ודעתו שאף טעם זה אמת הוא וראוי לאומרו. ונראה עוד דאף לפי טעם הרמב״ם אין העבודה רק להוציא מטעות אומות העולם, דודאי כל מה שאמר הרמב״ן דעבודת הקרבנות מועיל להוריד השכינה הוא אמת אף לפי טעם הרמב״ם. אלא נראה דעתו דהיה דרך אחר לפעול זאת, והקב״ה בחר זאת העבודה כדי להרחיקם מטעות עובדי ע״ז.

עוד תפש עליו הרמב״ן במה שפירש שמה שאירע באברהם אבינו בפרשת וירא היה רק מראה נבואה. ונראה בדעת הרמב״ם דאדרבה הרי מראה נבואה הוא יותר אמיתי ממה שאדם רואה ומרגיש בחוש וא״כ מה שאמר שהיה הכל במראה נבואה הרי זה בפועל כמו אם היה ממש בחוש. ומה שתפש עליו הרמב״ן דאיך היה יעקב אבינו צולע על יריכו אם מלחמתו עם המלאך היה רק במראה נבואה, לענ״ד דאין זה קושיא כלל דאם במראה נבואה ראה שיש שליטה לשרו של עשו לנגוע בכף יריכו, אין כאן תמיה שזה יפעול על החומריות, ומה שאירע למעלה הוא אמיתי ופועל על כל עניני עוה״ז. סוף דבר אף שיש מהלכים בספר מ״נ שאנו חולקים עליו ותופשים דרך הרמב״ן, מ״מ צריך לידע שהוא ספר קדוש נכתב מאיש קדוש שקבע יסודות ישרות באמונה ובטחון בכלל ישראל. ועוד ידוע שביאר

הרמב״ם בספרו, ענין אחדות הי״ת ופתח בו דרכים עמוקים בענין אמונה. ונתקבל בכלל ישראל.

והי״ת יסייענו שנגיע לסוף כוונת הרמב״ם בכתביו הקדושים, ונגיע למדרגת אמונה ובטחון שנזכר בספרו הלכות תשובה פ׳ י׳ הל׳ ב׳ עובד מאהבה עוסק בתורה ובמצות והולך בנתיבות החכמה לא מפני דבר בעולם ולא מפני יראת הרעה ולא כדי לירש הטובה אלא עושה האמת מפני שהוא אמת וסוף הטובה לבא בגללה, ומעלה זו היא מעלה גדולה מאד ואין כל חכם זוכה לה, והיא מעלת אברהם אבינו שקראו הקדוש ברוך הוא אוהבו לפי שלא עבד אלא מאהבה והיא המעלה שצונו בה הקדוש ברוך הוא על ידי משה שנאמר ואהבת את ה׳ אלהיך, ובזמן שיאהוב אדם את ה׳ אהבה הראויה מיד יעשה כל המצות מאהבה.

SUMMARY OF RABBI YAAKOV SCHNAIDMAN'S PROLOGUE

The Rambam begins Mishneh Torah, his monumental work detailing all the laws in the Torah, with an ethical introduction and the laws of character traits, because proper character traits are a prerequisite for Torah study. One who lacks these traits does not accomplish anything with his Torah learning, and even worse, may misconstrue the Torah to prove his false ideologies. Indeed, our sages tell us that Elisha ben Avuya became a sinner because his father taught him Torah for ulterior motives.

Just as Torah true character traits and ethics are a prerequisite to Torah study, so too must one believe and trust in Hashem and his Torah. If one's fundamental beliefs and trust in Hashem are lacking, and he doesn't study Torah as it was handed down by tradition, he is in grave danger of being led astray. This is especially true in our times. Moreh Nevuchim teaches fundamental beliefs and the proper way to understand the Torah.

There are many areas where our Torah tradition follows the Ramban's opinion rather than the Rambam's opinion as stated in Moreh Nevuchim. For example the Rambam writes that the purpose of *korbanos* is to counter idolatry, to which the Ramban writes, "These are meaningless words, making light of a serious question, and making the table of Hashem loathsome, suggesting [that *korbanos* are only meant to be] a demonstration against wicked and foolish individuals, while the Torah says that *korbanos* are the food of the fire, for a satisfying aroma."

Yet, the Rambam did not mean this was the ultimate purpose of *korbanos,* for he himself writes in Mishneh Torah, "All the *korbanos* are included in the category of *chukim* – mitzvos whose reasons are unfathomable. Our sages said that the world exists because of *kor-*

Rabbi Yaakov Schnaidman is the Rosh Yeshivah of Yeshivath Beth Moshe Scranton, Pennsylvania.

banos, because by doing *chukim* and *mishpatim* the righteous merit the World to Come. The Torah gave precedence to *chukim* as the verse says, *Heed My chukim and mishpatim, which man will do and live [eternally.]*" Rather, the Rambam, as well as other early commentators who gave reasons for the mitzvos, did not intend to give the ultimate reason for the mitzvah; they offered reasons in order to encourage mitzvah observance. Moreover, explaining the reasons for mitzvos is included in the mitzvah of Torah study.

Like the Ramban, the Rambam agreed that the primary purpose of *korbanos* was to bring the Shechinah down to us, but this could have been achieved through other methods. Sacrifices were chosen in order to counter idolatry. The Ramban understood that the Rambam's intention was not to explain the ultimate reason for the mitzvah, yet he disagreed with the Rambam's explanation on any level.

The Rambam also wrote that the three angels that appeared to Avraham, and the fight Yaakov had with the angel, were prophetic visions. The Ramban disagrees, proving his point from the fact that after Yaakov fought with the angel and was stricken in his thigh, he actually limped. However, the Rambam opines that something that happens in a prophetic vision is no less real than an actual event. Since he was hurt by the angel in his prophetic vision, he suffered a physical ailment in this world.

Although we follow the opinion of the Ramban, disagreeing with parts of Moreh Nevuchim, it is a holy sefer written by a holy author, who established fundamental principles of faith and trust for Yisrael.

May Hashem grant that we understand the ultimate intention of the writings of the Rambam, attaining the level of faith and trust mentioned in the Rambam at the end of the laws of teshuvah. "A person who serves G-d out of love busies himself Torah study and mitzvos, following the path of wisdom for the sake of the truth, and in the end, goodness will be granted to him because of his [virtuous mindset.] He does not fear G-d for selfish reasons, neither because he fears something bad will happen, nor to gain advantage. . . . G-d commanded us through Moshe [to serve Him] with love, as it says, *Love G-d, your Lord.* When one loves G-d properly, he immediately fulfills the mitzvos out of love."

TRANSLATOR'S INTRODUCTION

Moreh Nevuchim, one of the foremost works on Torah outlook of all time, was written by Rambam (Rabbi Moshe ben Maimon, 1135-1204) about 1185. It was written in Arabic, the language of the Jews of Egypt where Rambam lived, and subsequently translated into Hebrew by Rabbi Shemuel ibn Tibbon.

Rambam wrote *Moreh Nevuchim* for the benefit of intellectuals of his time who were confused by the writings of the Greek philosophers whose ideology was sharply at odds with the teachings of the Torah. For example, he refutes Aristotle's mistaken theory that the universe had no beginning and always existed, offering conclusive evidence that G-d created the world *yesh me'ayin*, "something from nothing," or "existence from non-existence."

But Moreh Nevuchim does much more than discredit false doctrines. Its pages offer a wealth of instruction and inspiration for every thinking Jew as they expound on such fundamental concepts as the Existence of G-d, His Oneness, His incorporeality, Divine Providence, the messianic age, resurrection, prophecy, and the reason for the mitzvos.

The present volume covers Part III, chapters 26 to 54 of *Moreh Nevuchim* which forms the conclusion and climax of the entire work. Here the Rambam explores the reason and purpose of the 613 mitzvos of the Torah. Additionally, he explains the significance of the narratives and chronologies in the Torah, shows the perfect way of praying, describes the perfect man, and much, much more.

The Rambam goes to great lengths in explaining the reasons for the *avodas hakorbanos*, (the laws of the offerings,) presenting a unique rationalization for this difficult subject. However, his views are harshly criticized by the Ramban (Nachmanides) in his commentary on *Vayikra* 1:9 where he offers his own reason for the *korbanos.* In order to offer the Ramban's alternative approach, his remarks have been included in this volume in the hope that the juxtaposition of the diverging views of these *gedolei olam* will shed light on this complex topic.

Moreh Nevuchim culminates in the idea that man reaches perfection by acquiring the knowledge of G-d and gaining the understanding that G-d oversees the actions and conduct of all mankind. Having attained the knowledge of G-d, this person will attempt to follow G-d's ways, leading his life with kindness, justice, and righteousness.

Rambam was born in 1135, in Cordova, Spain, a scion of a prominent family that traces its ancestry to Rabbi Yehudah haNasi, the compiler of the Mishnah. When he was 13 years old, Cordova was overrun by the Almohads, a fanatic Moslem sect from northern Africa. The ruthless invaders gave the Jewish community the choice between conversion to Islam, exile, or a martyr's death. Rambam's family, along with most other Jews fled the country, wandering about for twelve years, ultimately locating in Fez, Morocco. After a brief stay in Eretz Yisrael, Rambam settled in Fostat, near Cairo. Recognizing his prodigious scholarship, leadership qualities, and compassionate personality, the Cairo *kehillah* elected him as their chief rabbi and designated him *nagid* of the entire Jewish community of Egypt. Unwilling to derive benefit from his Torah knowledge, Rambam took up the study of medicine. Before long, he gained renown as a masterful healer and was appointed physician to the court of Sultan Saladin of Cairo.

It is my fervent hope that this translation will serve to inspire the reader with *ahavas Torah* and *yir'as Shamayim. Ki heim chayeinu ve'orech yameinu*, "For they are our life and the length of our days."

AVRAHAM YAAKOV FINKEL
Elul 5771/'11

MOREH NEVUCHIM

The Mitzvos

Chapter Twenty-six

The Reasons for the Mitzvos

Just as Torah scholars debate whether G-d's actions stem from His wisdom or only from His will, so do they differ concerning His mitzvos. Some scholars do not attempt to find a reason for the mitzvos at all, believing they are simply commanded by the will of G-d. Others maintain that all mitzvos and prohibitions emanate from G-d's wisdom; they are meant to fulfill a definite purpose with a beneficial reason for every mitzvah. [However, although] there is a reason for every mitzvah, we are not intelligent enough to understand the wisdom of some of the mitzvos. This [latter] opinion is the belief of all of us, common folk as well as scholars.

The verses in Scripture support the idea [that the mitzvos have reasons,] as it says, *[What nation has such] righteous rules and laws* (*Devarim* 4:8), and, *The judgments of Hashem are true, altogether righteous* (*Tehillim* 11:10).

Chukim and Mishpatim

One group of commandments is called *chukim*—decrees, [a word which] implies that there is no reason for the command. These include prohibitions such as *shaatneiz* [wearing garments made of wool combined with linen], cooking meat and milk together, and sending the goat into the wilderness on Yom Kippur. The Sages exhorted [Bnei Yisrael] about these mitzvos, saying, "Although the evil impulse makes you complain about these [incomprehensible] laws, and the nations of the world taunt you about them, you are not allowed to criticize them." The majority of our Sages did not believe these mitzvos have no reason and serve no purpose, for this would imply that G-d's actions are pointless. Rather, they believed [the *chukim*] do indeed have beneficial purpose, however due to our lack of knowledge and inadequate wisdom we do not know what it is.

Thus we can say there is a reason for every positive or negative mitzvah.[1] The benefit of some of the mitzvos, like the prohibitions of murder and theft, is obvious. The purpose of others, such as the prohibition of *orlah*—eating the fruit of a tree in the first three years (*Vayikra* 19:23), or *k'lai hakerem*—the fruit of a vineyard in which other seeds have grown (*Devarim* 22:9), is not so apparent.

The usefulness of a second group of mitzvos called *mishpatim*—judgments, is plainly evident, as opposed to *chukim*—decrees whose purpose is not understood. Referring to [the chukim] the Rabbis often quote the verse, [The *Torah*] *is not an empty thing from you* (*Devarim* 32:47), commenting: "It is not empty, but if it [seems] empty, it is only from you." In other words: These mitzvos are not empty things that have no useful purpose, rather, if you find a mitzvah that appears to be an empty teaching, it is *from you*, due to your lack of understanding.

Shelomoh knew the reason for all the mitzvos, except that of the *red heifer* (*Bamidbar* 19:2). Our Sages said G-d concealed the reasons for the mitzvos so people should not be lax with them, as Shelomoh did with two mitzvos whose reasons are clearly stated in the Torah.[2]

A Perplexing Midrash

The idea [that the mitzvos have reasons], is stated by the Rabbis and confirmed by Torah verses. However, I found one midrash

---

1 A positive mitzvah is something one must do; a negative mitzvah is something one is forbidden to do.

2 The Torah says *[the king] shall not have too many wives, so that his heart will not turn astray* (*Devarim* 17:17). Said Shelomoh, "I will have many wives, and I will not turn astray." However, in the end his wives led him astray. Furthermore, it says, *[The king] shall not have too many horses for himself, so that he will not return the people to Egypt* (ibid. v.16). Shelomoh said, "I will amass horses, and I will not return to Egypt." Yet in the end his chariots returned to Egypt (*Sanhedrin* 21b).

in *Bereishis Rabbah* that seems to suggest that some mitzvos have no purpose other than as a commandment from G-d. The midrash asks: Why does G-d care if an animal is killed by cutting the neck from the front or from the back? The midrash then answers: The mitzvos were only given to refine the Jewish people [testing if they would fulfill a mitzvah that is bewildering], as it says, *The word of Hashem purifies* (*Tehillim* 18:31).

This Midrash is unique; there is nothing in the writings of the Sages that compares to it. Nevertheless, my explanation is in consonance with the Rabbis who say that the mitzvos serve a useful purpose, as it says, *for [the Torah] is not an empty thing for you,* and, *I did not tell the descendants of Yaakov to seek Me for nothing. I am Hashem Who speaks righteousness, Who declares upright things* (*Yeshayah* 45:19).

I propose, and every intelligent person should believe, that every mitzvah was given for a reason and provides a benefit, however the details of the mitzvah [may serve no purpose other than to be fulfilled for the sake of the mitzvah.] For example: Killing animals in order to obtain good food is obviously a useful thing. However, stipulations such as killing the animal only through *shechitah*, which entails cutting the esophagus and the windpipe in a certain place [on the neck] and prohibiting *nechirah* [piercing] were given to refine the Jewish people [testing whether they will comply with the will of G-d.] With this explanation, one can understand the midrash which said [there is no difference between] killing an animal by cutting the neck from the front or the back.

The Sages used this example, [but actually, even the details of the laws of *shechitah* have a valid reason] which is to produce a painless and efficient slaughter. *Shechitah* is efficient because, severing the neck from the back requires a sword or a similar device, while *shechitah* can be done with any cutting tool. Our Sages demanded that a sharply honed knife be used in order to achieve an almost painless death.

A more fitting analogy can be found in the laws of the sacrifices. The mitzvah of offering sacrifices brings great benefits to man, and I will explain that later. But the specific details of why one offering should be a lamb, while another should be a ram, and why a certain number of each should be brought is inexplicable. Only a fool would attempt to find reasons for these specific regulations. Instead of removing obscurity, he is adding even more difficulties, [for the details of the sacrifice laws have no reason.] In fact, those who believe the [details] of the law have underlying reasons are as far removed from the truth as those who think the entire law [of offerings] is pointless.

G-d's wisdom demanded these specifics, but it is inevitable that some details of the mitzvos have no reasons. One might ask why a lamb is offered rather than a ram, and the same question could be asked if a ram were brought rather than a lamb. Similarly, one could ask why seven lambs rather than eight, ten, twenty, or any number [of animals] were brought? This is like asking why something has a certain shape rather than an infinite number of other possible shapes.

When the Rabbis said every mitzvah has a reason, and Shelomoh knew them all, they meant the basic mitzvah, rather than every minute detail, had a reason.

> **RAMBAN** *(Devarim 22:6): The Aggados that the Rambam found difficult, [which seem to indicate that there are no reasons for the mitzvos], have a different meaning. I think they imply that the commandments do not benefit the Holy One, blessed be He, but do benefit man, protecting him from harm, evil beliefs, and vile character traits. Their purpose may be to remind us of the miracles and wonders of the Creator, so we know G-d. This is the intent of the above-mentioned Midrash (Bereishis Rabbah 44:1): "The only reason for the mitzvos is to refine people," so they become pure like refined silver. [The jeweler] who refines silver does not do so without purpose, rather he removes any impurity. So too, the mitzvos remove false beliefs from our hearts, showing us the truth and helping us remember it forever.*

The above-cited Aggadah is also mentioned in Tanchuma (Shemini 8): "What difference does it make to the Holy One, blessed be He, whether one eats an animal that was slaughtered through shechitah or piercing? Do you help Him or harm Him in any way? Or what difference does it make to Him whether you eat clean or unclean animals? But, if you have become wise, you have become wise for your own good (Mishlei *9:12). So you see, the only reason the mitzvos were given is to refine people, as it says,* The words of Hashem are pure words (Tehillim *12:7), and,* Every word of G-d is refined (Mishlei *30:5). Why? So that [His word] should protect you." End of the text of Tanchuma.*

Here, the Rabbis explicitly tell us that the commandments were not given for the benefit of G-d, although one might think that the Menorah was made because G-d needs light, or that G-d needs the sacrifices for food or the burning of the incense for fragrance. Even the commandments to remember the miracles He performed at the Exodus and Creation were not given for G-d's benefit, rather so that we should know the truth and thereby be worthy of G-d's protection. Our veneration and our remembrance of His wonders mean nothing to Him.

[The law delineating] that slaughter must be done by cutting the front not the back of the neck or by piercing the animal proves that we, not G-d, benefit from the commandments. It is impossible to say that the Creator derives more glory when shechitah is done from the throat rather than from the back of the neck, or by piercing the animal. Rather, the commandments were given for our benefit, to make us compassionate even when we slaughter the animal.

The Rabbis bring another proof: What difference does it make to G-d whether we eat pure animals—that is, permissible food, or impure animals—forbidden foods, about which the Torah says, They are unclean to you (Vayikra *11:26). They are only forbidden so we can attain a pure soul, becoming wise men who discern the truth.*

The Rabbis quoted the verse, If you have become wise, you have become wise for your own good, telling us that the commandments that define actions, such as shechitah by cutting the throat, are designed to teach us good character traits. The commandments delineating which animals [may be eaten] purify our souls, as the Torah says, Do not make yourselves disgusting through animals, birds or anything that creeps on the ground that I have separated out for you as being unclean (Vayikra *20:25). Therefore, all the commandments are solely for our benefit, as Elihu said,* If you have sinned, how have you affected Him? If your transgressions multiply, what have you done to Him? If you were righteous what have you given Him, or what has He taken from your hand? (Iyov *35:6,7). All the Rabbis agree on this point.*

Plan for Classification of Mitzvos

I classified the six hundred and thirteen mitzvos into categories, each containing many mitzvos of the same or similar variety. I will first explain the reason for each category and its true purpose, and then I will explain the reason for each individual mitzvah. I have also been able to understand the reason for the details of some of the mitzvos. I have not explained a small number of mitzvos, since those reasons have eluded me until today. Allow me to preface these explanations with the following introduction.

Chapter Twenty-seven

Physical and Spiritual Perfection

The Torah has a two-fold purpose: to foster both spiritual and physical well-being. Spiritual well-being is achieved when proper beliefs that can be grasped by the masses are transmitted. Some of these beliefs are conveyed explicitly, while others, which are difficult for common people to understand when presented literally, are conveyed in a figurative manner.

Physical well-being is achieved when people live civilly with one another, which is accomplished by promoting equity and adopting moral values. In a fair society, everyone yields to the common good, rather than doing as they please and having their way by force. Good moral values ensure a smooth-running society.

Spiritual well-being, [merited] through proper beliefs, is by far the more important of the two goals; however physical well-being, with an efficient government and good relations between people, precedes the first in nature and in time. Because spiritual well-being can only be achieved after physical well-being, the Torah deals with physical well-being carefully and painstakingly. Man has a dual perfection: that of the body and that of the soul. With physical perfection, man is in the best of health, and all his needs, including food, shelter, bathing facilities, and the like are fulfilled. It is impossible for someone who lives in seclusion to acquire all these necessities; he can only procure them by living in a community, especially since man is social-minded by nature.

Superiority of Spiritual Perfection

Man's ultimate perfection is to be a thinking being; knowing all there is to know about the things in existence. This knowledge, which is attained through reasoning and validated through research and testing, does not include any actions or moral qualities.

Someone who suffers from hunger, thirst, heat or cold cannot grasp an idea, even if it is explained to him, and he surely cannot originate an idea by his own reasoning. Therefore, the higher degree of perfection can be attained only after the first perfection [of physical well-being] has been satisfied. Only after achieving the first perfection, can man attain the second perfection which is the loftier of the two and the source of eternal life.

The one and only true Torah, given to us by Moshe Rabbeinu, helps us achieve both perfections. With the establishment of good interpersonal relations, repressing wrongdoing and adopting virtuous character traits, the population of every country can live securely and the first perfection [of physical well-being] is acquired. [The Torah also trains us] in matters of faith, teaching correct and true beliefs through which the ultimate [spiritual] perfection can be achieved.

The purpose of the entire Torah is for man to achieve both perfections, as it says, *Hashem commanded us to keep all these rules, so that we would remain in awe of Hashem for all time, for our good always, so that we would survive even as we are today* (*Devarim* 6:24). The second perfection, expressed in the words *for our good always,* is mentioned first because it is of greater importance, being the ultimate goal of man's existence. Our Sages expound the verse, *[If you do this,] you will have it good and will live long* (ibid. 22:7) thusly: *You will have it good* in the world that is all good; *and will live long* in the world that is everlasting. Similarly, the phrase, *for our good always* means we may come into the world that is all good and everlasting where we may live eternally. The words, *so that we would survive even as we are today* refer to our physical existence which lasts for a limited time, and can only be peaceful and serene if people cooperate with one another.

Chapter Twenty-eight

Fundamental Mitzvos

The Existence of G-d, His Oneness, that He is All-Knowing, His Power, His Will, and the Eternity of G-d are the fundamental beliefs through which man's ultimate perfection is attained; they are mentioned in the Torah explicitly. The Torah commands belief in the fundamental principles, however the prerequisite ideas necessary [to fully understand them] are not expressed in the Torah; they only can be inferred through extensive research. The Torah also teaches us fundamental beliefs necessary for a society, such as believing G-d's anger is aroused against those who rebel against Him, for thereby we will be in awe of Him, fear Him, and obey Him.

There are also cosmic truths established by science, that are necessary prerequisites to understand the fundamental beliefs. These truths are not mentioned explicitly in the Torah, rather, the Torah commands us to love Hashem in the verse *Love Hashem your G-d with all your heart, with all your soul, and with all your might* (Devarim 6:5), yet this love can only be actualized if one is aware of the marvels of nature and contemplates G-d's wisdom evident in the wonders of the universe. We discussed this in *Mishneh Torah* (*Hilchos Yesodei Hatorah*, ch. 2), also mentioning what our Sages commented on this subject.

Mitzvos that Need Explanation

These preliminary remarks underscore that when the positive and negative mitzvos prevent crime, promote the well-being of the community through good conduct, or teach fundamental doctrines, their reasons and benefit are obvious. Some of the fundamental beliefs are important in and of themselves, while others are necessary to remove injustice or teach good character traits. No one can doubt why we must believe G-d is One; or why we are forbidden to kill, steal, take revenge, or retaliate; or why we are commanded to love one another.

The mitzvos about which people disagree, some believing they serve no purpose, others believing their purpose is hidden from man, are those mitzvos which do not seem to advance any of the three benefits we have mentioned. They do not seem to convey any teaching, inspire people to reach for higher moral levels, or prevent injustice. In other words, these mitzvos do not seem to improve the well-being of the soul by teaching any moral lesson; or the well-being of the body by establishing rules useful for a government or family household to function. These mitzvos include the prohibitions of *shaatneiz* (wearing a garment made of wool combined with linen), *kilayim* (sowing mixed seeds), boiling meat and milk together, the mitzvos of *kisuy hadam* (covering the blood of slaughtered birds and non-domestic animals), *eglah arufah* (breaking the neck of a calf when a murder victim is found slain by an unknown killer), *peter chamor* (redeeming a firstborn donkey), and others like these. Further in this book I explain these mitzvos and delineate reasons for them, except for some details of mitzvos, as I have mentioned.

Indeed, these and similar mitzvos do promote correct beliefs and improve social relations by preventing injustice and teaching moral values. Correct beliefs include such cases where the belief itself is the purpose of that mitzvah, such as the belief in G-d's Oneness, G-d's eternity, and His in-corporeality. Other beliefs are only important because they help remove injustice or adopt moral character traits, such as the belief that G-d is angry with those who oppress their fellowmen, as it says, *I will then display My anger and kill you by the sword* (*Shemos* 22:23); or the belief that G-d hears the crying of the oppressed, to deliver them out of the hands of the oppressor, as it says, *Therefore, if he cries to Me, I will listen, for I am compassionate* (ibid. 22:26).

Chapter Twenty-nine

The Scourge of Idolatry

Our father Avraham was brought up in the environment of the [idolatrous] Sabean faith. From their scriptures and ancient chronicles, which are available in Arabic translation, and which I will relate to you in this chapter, you will realize that they worshiped the stars.[3] They believed that the seven moving stars were gods, but the sun and the moon were greater than the five other stars. Indeed, they considered the sun to be their supreme deity, governing both the upper and lower worlds.

In these chronicles they forged the history of Avraham our father, recording the following story. Avraham was raised in Kuta. When he argued with the people, claiming there was a Creator other than the sun, they countered with the indisputable effect the sun has on the cosmos. "You are right," replied Avraham, "but the sun is merely like an ax in the hands of a wood chopper."

Avraham's arguments against his opponents circulated, and finally the king imprisoned him for a long time. Even while in prison Avraham continued to assert his viewpoint, disputing the people's arguments. Eventually the king, fearing that [Avraham] would undermine his regime by turning the people away from their religion, banished him to the Far East, confiscating all his assets.

This story, found in a book called The Nabatean Agriculture, does not report what is related in our Torah, nor does it mention the prophetic revelation [Avraham] received. The authors left out these things because he attacked their evil doctrine. I do not doubt

3 The Rambam relates the beliefs and practices of the pagans of Avraham's time to demonstrate that the purpose of many mitzvos is to counteract idolatrous beliefs and practices.

that he was cursed, despised, and held in contempt by these misguided folks for criticizing their beliefs. [As a reward] for enduring [this humiliation] for the sake of G-d—as he rightly did—G-d said to him, *I will bless those who bless you, and he who curses you I will curse* (*Bereishis* 12:3).

Avraham's success is manifested by the fact that today, even people who are not his descendants aspire to be [spiritually] connected to him, praising him and wishing to be blessed by him. Only the remnants of the Sabean nation that once filled the earth, like the vulgar Turks in the far north and the Indians in the far south, oppose him and deny his eminence.

Bizarre Sabean Tales

Philosophers in those days thought G-d was the spirit of the spheres and stars, which are physical bodies. Abu-bakr al Zaig mentions this in his commentary on the Book of Physics.

Since the Sabeans believed that heaven was god, they believed that the universe always existed. They claimed that Adam, like all other people, was a human born of a father and mother, but they lauded him as a prophet of the moon, summoning people to worship the moon. In addition, they said he wrote essays on agriculture.

According to the Sabeans, Noach was a farmer who did not approve of idol worship. The Sabeans faulted him for this, imprisoning him for worshipping G-d. They tell many other tales about him in their books.

The Sabeans concocted ridiculous stories about Sheis, Adam's son, claiming that he disagreed with his father about worshipping the moon. Their writings prove that the authors were fools who knew nothing about philosophy.

There are many more absurd Sabeans tales. They describe how Adam left the hot climate of India for Babylon, bringing with him fantastical things, such as a golden tree that grew leaves and branches, a stone tree, a fresh leaf of a fire-proof tree, and two leaves from another tree that could each cover two men. He told of a tree that was the height of a man, yet could shelter ten thousand men.

I am surprised that people who think the universe always existed believe in stories such as these, since any student of natural science knows they contradict the laws of nature. But they tell these stories about Adam to support their theory of the eternity of the universe, which is basic to the belief that the stars and spheres are deities.

[Avraham,] the "Pillar of the World", was convinced that there is an intangible Divine Being that is neither a body nor a force within a body, and all the spheres and stars are His creations. Realizing that the foolish tales of the day were lies, he decried their religion, impressing upon the Sabeans the falsehood of their doctrines. He spoke out against them, proclaiming *the name of Hashem, the G-d of the universe* (*Bereishis* 21:33), declaring both the existence of G-d, and that He is the Creator of the universe.

The Sabeans, in accordance with their beliefs, erected statues to the stars, silver statues to the moon, and golden statues to the sun. Because they attributed the different climates to the stars, believing that specific stars were the gods of specific climates, they built temples and placed their statues in them. They trusted that the influence of the stars would flow down to these statues, enabling them to give prophetic inspiration to people, telling them what is beneficial for them.

Similarly, they felt trees dedicated to a star and planted in honor of that star, were under its domain. The spiritual force of the star rested on that tree, speaking to the people through prophecy while they slept. These beliefs are recorded in their books.

The people who subscribed to these beliefs are recorded in Tanach as the prophets of Baal and Ashtaros. Brainwashed by the Sabean doctrine, they abandoned G-d and cried out, "*Baal, please hear us!*" (1 *Melachim* 18:16). This religion was popular at that time. Ignorance was widespread, and the world was fascinated with Sabean mania, giving rise to occult beliefs and to practitioners who divined auspicious times and omens, practiced witchcraft, used incantations, consulted mediums and oracles, and attempted to communicate with the dead.

Purpose of the Mitzvos

In *Mishneh Torah* we show that Avraham was the first to discredit this ideology with gentle arguments and persuasive words. Treating people kindly, he convinced them to worship Hashem. Only later, did [Moshe,] the greatest of all prophets, complete [Avraham's] work by commanding that these unbelievers be put to death, with their memory blotted out and uprooted from "the land of the living," as it says, *You must shatter their altars, break down their sacred pillars, and cut down their Asheirah trees* (*Shemos* 34:13). He prohibited us from following their ways, as it says, *Do not follow the customs of the nations that I am driving out before you* (*Vayikra* 20:23).

From the numerous passages in the Torah [forbidding idolatry] we understand that the main purpose of the mitzvos of the Torah is the total destruction of idolatry and anything associated with it. Even the mention of its name and any practice that smacks of idolatry, such as divining auspicious times and omens, practicing witchcraft, using incantations, consulting mediums and oracles, or attempting to communicate with the dead, is prohibited.

The Torah forbids us to copy the ways of the heathens, much less to join them. The Torah explicitly states that whatever idolaters consider a service to their gods and a means of getting close to them is despised by Hashem, as it says, *In worshiping their gods [these nations] committed all sorts of perversions hated by Hashem* (*Devarim* 12:31).

Their books record that on certain occasions they offered seven beetles, seven mice, and seven bats to the sun, their greatest god, certainly something to disgust a person. All the mitzvos that forbid idolatry and everything connected with it, leading to it, or related to it, have an obvious purpose—they are meant to save us from the evil beliefs which surrounded our fathers and forefathers, as it says, *Thus said Hashem the G-d of Yisrael. Your forefathers—Terach, the father of Avraham and the father of Nachor—always dwelt beyond the [Euphrates] River, and they served other gods* (*Yehoshua* 24:2).

Speaking about these [idolatrous] doctrines, the true prophets declared, *They walked after vain things that do not profit* (1 *Shemuel* 12:21).

How beneficial is every mitzvah that saves us from this great error, leading us back to the correct belief that G-d, the Creator of all things, rules the universe and only He, rather than those fictitious deities, must be served, loved, and feared. Approaching the true G-d and gaining His favor does not involve any hardship. The only requirement is to love and fear Him; this is the purpose of serving G-d, as it says, *And now, Yisrael, what does Hashem want of you? Only that you fear Hashem your G-d, so that you will follow all His paths and love Him, serving Hashem your G-d with all your heart and with all your soul* (*Devarim* 10:12). Later, I will discuss this subject in depth.

Guidebook of Idol Worship

My knowledge of the belief, rituals, and worship of the Sabeans helped me understand the reason for many of our mitzvos, as you will see when I explain mitzvos that seem to have no purpose. By sourcing my information about the Sabean religion and ideology, you can rest assured my theory about the mitzvos is correct.

The most important book on this subject is The Nabatean Agriculture, translated by Ibn Vach'shiya. In chapter 30 I will explain why the Sabeans recorded their religious doctrine in a book about agriculture. This book is full of the idolaters' drivel about things that fascinate common people, such as amulets, conjuring up spirits, witchcraft, demons, and ghosts that live in the desert. The book also contains ludicrous comments, scorned by intelligent people, which belittle the open miracles that help people recognize that there is a G-d who is the Judge of all mankind, as it says, *You will then know that the whole world belongs to G-d* (*Shemos* 9:29), and, *You will then realize that I am Hashem, right here on earth* (ibid. 9:18).

Bizarre Tales

The book claims that Adam wrote about a tree found in India, whose branches, if thrown on the ground, creep along like snakes. Another tree has a root shaped like a man which makes sounds and speaks a series of words. [Adam's book] also mentions a plant whose leaf makes a person invisible when it is placed in his pocket, enabling him to enter and leave a place without being seen. If any part of this plant is burnt in open air, a thunderous noise is heard while the smoke rises. Many more fairy tales like this are used to teach the wonders of plants and methods of agricultural techniques in order to cast doubt on the miracles [of the Torah], suggesting that [those wonders] were done by illusion and sleight of hand.

Another fairy tale relates that the althea tree, one of the *asheiros* they used to worship, stood in Nineveh for twelve thousand years. The althea fought with the mandrake plant because the mandrake wanted to take its place. One man who received prophetic messages from the [althea] tree stopped receiving messages for while. When the prophetic messages returned, the althea explained that it had been involved in an argument with the mandrake. [The althea] ordered him to write to the Chaldean sorcerers, asking them to decide whether the althea or mandrake was better and more effective for witchcraft. This long story reveals the mindset and level of education of the people of that time.

Such were the wise men of Babylon in the dark ages referred to in Tanach, and these were the religious beliefs they held. Were it not that belief in the existence of G-d is universally accepted today, our current situation would be even darker than those days, albeit in different ways.

The Tall Tale of Tammuz

The following story is related in The Nabatean Agriculture: A pagan prophet named Tammuz urged the king to worship the seven planets and twelve constellations of the zodiac. Thereupon the king killed him in a gruesome manner. On the night of his death the [idolatrous] statues from all over the world gathered in the temple of Babylon, at the site of the great golden statue dedicated to the sun.

This statue, which was suspended between heaven and earth, descended to eulogize Tammuz. Surrounded by the other statues it described what happened to him, and all the statues cried and mourned the entire night. At dawn they flew back to their temples in the four corners of the earth. This [event] is the source of the custom that women weep and mourn for Tammuz on the first day of the month of Tammuz.[4]

The story of Tammuz is a deep-rooted part of the ancient Sabean culture. The book reveals most of the warped ideas, practices, and festivals of the Sabeans.

A Warning

Do not think there is any truth to the stories they tell about Adam and the serpent, the tree of knowledge of good and evil, and the allusion that he was not used to wearing clothing. Careful review will show you that these stories are forgeries, adapted from the Torah after it became known among the nations. They heard about the story of Creation, and understanding it only in its literal meaning, rewrote it to convince the ignorant that the world always existed [and was not created by G-d], to persuade them that the events described in the chapter of Creation happened the way they recorded them.

---

[4] See *Yechezkel* 8:14. The Tammuz was an idol made in such a way as to create the optical illusion that it was crying (Rashi).

You will not be deluded by the nonsense of the Sabeans and the Chaldeans who are uneducated in any of the true sciences, but I urge you to warn others, for ordinary people tend to believe such fairy tales. . . .

The Underlying Principle of the Torah

Because the central idea of the Torah is to eradicate [idolatrous] ideas from our hearts and remove its symbols from existence, knowledge of the Sabean doctrines and practices helps explain the reasons for the mitzvos. The mitzvah to wipe out pagan ideas is found in the verses, *Be careful that your heart not be tempted* (*Devarim* 11:16), and, *There must not be among you any man . . . whose heart strays from Hashem* (ibid. 29:17). The destruction of [the symbols of] idolatry is commanded in the verse, *You must tear down their altars, break down their sacred pillars, cut down their Asheirah trees, and burn their idols in fire* (ibid. 7:5), and, *You must obliterate their name* (ibid. 12:3). These two concepts are repeated frequently, forming the underlying principle of the entire Torah, as our Sages told us in their commentary on the words, *All that Hashem commanded you through Moshe* (*Bamidbar* 15:23). This verse teaches that whoever accepts idolatry is considered like one who denies the whole Torah, and whoever rejects idolatry is considered like one who follows the entire Torah (Kiddushin 40a).

Chapter Thirty

The Torah Combats Idolatry

These ancient doctrines reveal that most people believed the earth would become populated and the land fertile by worshipping the stars. Their pious men admonished them thus, preaching that agriculture, on which the people depended, would only thrive if they worshipped the sun and stars. If they angered [the gods] by rebelling against them, the land would be ravaged, becoming desolate.

Their books state that Mars became angry [with people and turned the land into] deserts and wasteland, making it an arid wilderness inhabited by demons. They praise ranchers and farmers who are engaged in farming, [the kind of work] favored by the stars. The idolaters valued oxen, not allowing them to be killed, because they were so important for tilling the soil, and because the [ox], in spite of its great strength, obeys man's orders, since the gods want it to work the farms. These beliefs were generally accepted, and idol worship became closely linked with agriculture, since agriculture is vital for the sustenance of man and most animals. The idolatrous priests preached that certain actions would bring rain, so the trees could bear fruit and the land would be fertile and populated. The Nabatean Agriculture states: All ancient wise men and prophets have given orders to play certain instruments before the statues during the festivals, explaining that the gods were pleased with this, richly rewarding those who do so with long life, protection from suffering, an end to sickness, and an abundant harvest of grain and fruit.

The Aim of the Torah

Hashem, in His great mercy, wishing to save us from misery, urged us to keep away from the widespread, useless [pagan] practices by giving us His Torah. Moshe told us in the name of Hashem that worshipping stars and statues would cause the rain to stop falling, destroying the land so nothing would grow and causing the fruit of the trees to shrivel. Calamities would strike the people, diseases would infect their bodies, and life would be shortened. This is the essence of the covenant that Hashem instructed Moshe to make with Bnei Yisrael (*Devarim* 28:69).

The Torah constantly reiterates that idol worship will cause drought, devastation of the land, bad times, sickness, and a shortened lifespan, while serving Hashem will bring abundant rain, causing the land to thrive, as well as bringing good times, health, and long life. [The Torah] emphasizes its message in contradistinction to the preaching of the idolatrous priests, since the primary aim of the Torah is to remove idolatry, obliterating it.

Chapter Thirty-one

The Purpose of the Mitzvos

Some people misguidedly say the mitzvos and prohibitions have no rational basis, thinking that if the mitzvos were given for a reason, it would be tantamount to saying they were not divinely inspired. Only commandments that do not make sense and serve no purpose undoubtedly emanate from G-d, because no human mind could produce them. These weak-minded people actually feel man is more perfect than his Creator, for man's actions have a purpose, but [according to them] G-d commands us to do things that are useless and forbids us to do things that are harmless.

G-d forbid! The purpose of the mitzvos is to benefit us, as it says, *Hashem commanded us to keep all these chukim-rules for our good* (*Devarim* 6:14), and, *The nations will hear all these chukim-rules and say, "This great nation is surely a wise and understanding people"* (ibid. 4:6). The verse explicitly states that even the *chukim* [laws, whose reasons are unfathomable] convince all the nations that they contain wisdom and understanding. If these rules had neither reason nor benefit and did not prevent harm, why would anyone think that those who follow them are wise, understanding, and worthy of universal admiration?

Undoubtedly, the aim of every one of the 613 mitzvos is to teach correct outlook, remove erroneous opinion, proclaim rule of justice, remove injustice, train good character traits, and warn against bad character traits. Thus, all the mitzvos deal with one of the following three categories: social harmony, character traits, and interpersonal relations.

Chapter Thirty-two

Gradual Advancement

G-d's wisdom is evident in the creation of animals, through the levels of motor development of their limbs, and the ways [the limbs] are connected to each other. You will further recognize His wisdom in the step-by-step maturation and over-all growth of the animal.

The brain exemplifies the levels of motor development and limb placement in an animal. The front lobe of the brain is very soft, the back lobe is a little harder, the marrow of the spine is still harder, and the farther the marrow extends into the spinal column the harder it becomes. The nerves are the organs of feeling and motion. The nerves needed for feeling or fine motor movements of the eyelids or jaw come from the brain. The nerves needed for gross motor movement of the limbs emerge from the spinal cord. . . . By this gradual development the nerves are capable of setting the limbs in motion.

This is only one example of the wonders described in the book On the Use of the Limbs.[5] These wonders are obvious to anyone probing them with an open mind.

Similarly, G-d provides food for mammals that are extremely tender at birth and unable to eat dry food. Milk giving breasts enable the mothers to nourish their young with milk; in this way the young animal is fed suitably moist food until it grows strong and its limbs become dry and hard.

---

5 Written by Galen, the most accomplished physician, surgeon, researcher, and philosopher of antiquity, died in Rome, ca. 217 c.e.

Many rules in our G-d-given Torah are based on the principle [of gradual advancement], because it is against human nature to shift abruptly from one extreme to the other.

Hashem sent Moshe to turn [the Jews from idol worshippers] into a *kingdom of kohanim and a holy nation* (*Shemos* 19:6) through the knowledge of G-d, as it says, *You are the ones who have been shown so that you will know that Hashem is the Supreme Being, and there is none beside Him* (*Devarim* 4:35), and, *Realize it today and ponder it in your heart, that Hashem is G-d in heaven above and on the earth beneath—there is no other* (ibid. v.19), and through devoting ourselves to His worship, as it says, *And to serve Him with all your heart* (ibid. 11:13), and, *You shall serve Hashem your G-d* (*Shemos* 23:25), and, *You shall serve Him* (*Devarim* 13:5).

The general pattern of worship in the world at that time involved sacrificing animals in the temples where images were set up, bowing down to those images, and placing incense before them. The devout men among the nations performed the service in these temples.

G-d in His wisdom did not command us to renounce these forms of worship because it would have been too difficult to accept such a command, as it is against human nature for man to abruptly stop what he is used to doing. The rejection of those forms of worship would have sounded [as absurd] then, as a prophet would sound today, were he to summon us to worship G-d in thought only, telling us not to pray to Him, nor fast, nor ask for His help in time of trouble.

Changing the Unholy into the Holy

Therefore, G-d allowed the kind of service [that was used by the idolaters] to continue, but He transformed the worship of man-made objects and figments of the imagination into service dedicated to His Name. He commanded us to build a temple, as it says, *They shall make Me a sanctuary* (*Shemos* 25:8), ordering the altar to be built for His name, as it says, *Make an earthen altar for Me* (ibid. 20:21), and the sacrifices to be offered to Him, as it says,

When one of you brings an offering to Hashem (*Vayikra* 1:2). He commanded that we bow down to Him, and burn incense for Him, and He prohibited any of these acts of worship to any other deity, as it says, *Whoever sacrifices to any deity other than G-d alone must be condemned to death* (*Shemos* 22:19), and, *Do not bow down to any other god* (ibid. 34:14). He singled out the kohanim for service in the Beis Hamikdash, as it says, *Sanctifying them to be kohanim to Me* (ibid. 28:41). He mandated gifts for the Levi'im and kohanim for their sustenance[6] since they perform the service in the Beis Hamikdash and bring the offerings. As a result of His Divine plan, eventually idolatry was discarded and the fundamental principle of our faith—the Existence and Oneness of Hashem—became firmly established. The [gradual] abolition of the people's [idolatrous] service did not dismay or disturb them.

A Question

You may wonder: How can we assume that mitzvos and prohibitions and important acts which are fully explained and must be done at prescribed times [of the year] were not commanded for their own sake but for the sake of something else? Are mitzvos only indirect steps devised by Hashem to achieve His primary goal? What prevented Him from making His primary goal a direct commandment for us, and giving us the ability to fulfill it? Then there would be no need for all the commandments [concerning temple service, sacrifices, and kohanim] which you suggest are only secondary steps toward the primary goal.

My answer will show you the truth of the subject. The following verse from the Torah illustrates the idea [of a primary goal being achieved through a secondary stage]: *G-d did not lead them through the Philistine highway, although it was the shorter route. G–d's consideration was that if the people encountered armed resistance, they would lose heart and return to Egypt. G-d therefore made*

6 The first tithe for the Levi'im, and 24 priestly gifts for the kohanim.

the people take a roundabout path by way of the desert to the Red Sea (*Shemos* 13:17,18).

G-d led the people on an indirect route, away from the highway He originally intended, because He was afraid they would be unable to endure the hardships of the highway. He led them by another road in order to accomplish His original intention.

Breaking the Addiction to Idolatry

In the same vein, G-d gave the commandments we mentioned above [such as building an altar, bringing sacrifices, etc.] for fear the Jews would not be able to refrain from the [religious] acts that were second nature to them.

These mitzvos achieve G-d's primary goal, that people should know that He exists and they should reject idolatry. But it goes against human nature for a person to suddenly cease all the different kinds of religious observances he is accustomed to doing which have become second nature to him, just as it goes against nature for a person who was brought up as a slave and worked with mortar and bricks all his life, to wash his dirty hands, and immediately [join an elite battalion and] fight against descendants of giant.

Similarly, Hashem led the Jews through the wilderness to make them bold and courageous. For it is a well-known fact that traveling in the wilderness without the comforts of home makes a man fearless; the opposite makes him timid and fainthearted. Additionally the generation born [in the wilderness] did not experience humiliation and slavery. The travels in the wilderness happened by order of G-d through Moshe, as it says, *They thus camped at Hashem's word and moved at Hashem's word, keeping their trust in Hashem's word. It was all done according to Hashem's word through Moshe* (*Bamidbar* 9:23).

This group of mitzvos [about temple service, offerings and kohanim] was given by Hashem to allow the people to continue the kind of worship they were used to doing. Thus, the true belief, G–d's primary intention, would become embedded in their consciousness.

More Questions

Why didn't G-d give us the ability to fulfill His primary goal, [after] making it an outright commandment? This leads to a parallel question: Why didn't G-d lead the Jews by way of the Philistine highway, giving them the ability to fight wars? [Had He done so] there would have been no need for the detour through the desert, with the pillar of cloud by day and the pillar of fire by night.

These queries beg a third question about reward for keeping the mitzvos and punishment for transgressing them. If it is G-d's primary goal that we believe in the Torah and fulfill the mitzvos, why not give us the ability to accept and fulfill it continually, instead of rewarding obedience and punishing rebelliousness? Since the promise of reward and the threat of punishment are simply a means to achieve His primary goal, what prevented G-d from instilling in us, as part of our nature, the will to do the things He wants us to do and reject the worship He despises?

There is one answer to these and all similar questions. Although G-d did change nature when He performed the miracles [mentioned in the Torah], He never performs a miracle by changing a person's character traits. Indeed, G-d Himself states this important principle in the following verse, *If only their hearts would always remain this way, where they are in such awe of Me* (*Devarim* 5:26).[7] It is for this reason that He gave us commandments, rewards and punishments.

It is not difficult for G-d to change a person's nature, but according to the principles laid down in the Torah, He does not wish to do so. Were He to change the nature of any person to enable that man to follow His will, the mission of the prophets and the giving of the mitzvos would be useless.[8]

---

[7] G-d wishes they would always be in awe of Him, but He does nothing to change their character.

[8] Because it would negate the principle of *bechirah chofshis*—free will.

Cutting Down on Sacrificial Service

Offering sacrifices is an indirect path toward G-d's primary goal [of believing in His Oneness and rejecting idolatry,] whereas prayer and supplication are indispensable tools to attain this goal. Therefore, the Torah distinguishes between these two kinds of service. Although sacrifices are offered to G-d, many regulations are connected to this service. Its performance was not permitted in every place and at all times, nor was it permitted to build a temple at will, nor could anyone become a priest at will to offer sacrifices. Only one temple was designated, as it says, *You must take [your offerings] and bring them to the place that Hashem shall choose* (*Devarim* 12:26), and sacrifices were precluded from being offered anywhere else, *in any place that you may see fit* (ibid. 12:13). Only members of a particular family [i.e., kohanim] were allowed to officiate as priests. These rules served to tone down this kind of worship, so only specific parts of the sacrificial service that G-d did not want abolished should remain. But prayer and supplication can be offered everywhere, by every person. This is also true for the mitzvos of *tzitzis, mezuzah, tefillin,* and similar kinds of divine service.

The prophets repeatedly reprimand the people for being too enthusiastic about offering sacrifices, explaining that sacrifices in and of themselves are not the main goal, and G-d does not need them.

Thus Shemuel said, *Does Hashem delight in elevation offerings and feast-offerings as in obedience to the voice of Hashem?* (1 *Shemuel* 15:22). Yeshayah exclaimed, *Why do I need your numerous sacrifices? Says Hashem* (*Yeshayah* 1:11). Yirmeyah declared, *For I did not speak with your forefathers, nor did I command them on the day I took them out of the land of Egypt concerning burnt or peace offerings. Rather, it was only this thing that I commanded them, saying, Hearken to My voice, then I will be your G-d, and you will be My people* (*Yirmeyah* 7:22,23).

Explanation of a Perplexing Passage

This statement of Yirmeyah has perplexed many people who ask: How can Yirmeyah say in the name of Hashem that He has not commanded us to bring burnt offerings and sacrifices? In fact, there are many mitzvos in the Torah dealing with this subject!

[Yirmeyah] is explaining that the primary purpose [for the mitzvos] is to know G-d and refrain from worshipping any other gods, thereby, *I will be your G-d and you will be My people.* The laws about sacrifices were given only as a means to reach this goal, and it is to that end that G-d shifted these [sacrificial] forms of worship to His name. As a result, all traces of idol worship would be obliterated, and belief in the Oneness of G-d would become firmly established.

[Speaking in G-d's name,] the prophet continues: But you have reversed the process, turning the means into the end. You have doubted My existence, *You have denied the providence of Hashem and said: It is not so* (*Yirmeyah* 5:12). *You worshiped idols, burnt incense to Baal and walked after gods of others that you never knew and then stand before Me in this Temple* (ibid. 7:9,10). And you continue visiting the House of Hashem offering sacrifices although this is not [My] primary purpose.

Furthermore, the Torah and our oral tradition state that in fact, the first mitzvos given to us were not about burnt offerings and sacrifices. The only exception is the Pesach offering in Egypt, which was brought for a specific reason that I will explain [in chapter 46.] Besides, this command was given in Egypt, while the laws referred to by Yirmeyah were given after the exodus from Egypt. For this reason [Yirmeyah] explicitly specifies, *on the day I took them out of the land of Egypt.*

Shabbos and Civil Laws

The first mitzvos after the exodus from Egypt were given at Marah, where Hashem said, *If you obey Hashem your G-d and do what is upright in His eyes, carefully heeding all His commandments and keeping all His decrees* (*Shemos* 15:26).

According to our tradition, Shabbos and civil laws were given at Marah, as the verse states: *There He established [for the nation] a decree and an ordinance* (ibid. v.25). *A decree* alludes to Shabbos, and *an ordinance* refers to civil laws which prevent injustice. The law of Shabbos confirms the fundamental principle that G-d created the world [out of nothing,] thus the commandment of [Shabbos] constitutes G-d's primary purpose for the mitzvos. In addition to implanting the correct ideology, G-d's primary purpose also includes preventing injustice; hence civil laws were also given immediately. Our first laws did not relate to burnt offerings or sacrifices, because these are only secondary goals.

This idea is also expressed in *Tehillim*, where people are admonished for ignoring G-d's primary purpose, failing to make a distinction between the primary and the secondary purposes. Asaf said, *Pay heed my people and I shall speak; Yisrael, and I shall bear witness against you; G-d, your G-d am I. I shall not rebuke you for your sacrifices, nor are your burnt-offerings my constant concern. I take not from your household any bull, nor from your pens any goats* (*Tehillim* 50:7-9).

RAMBAN *(Vayikra 1:9): But these are meaningless words, making light of a serious question [why Hashem needs man's offerings], and making the table of Hashem loathsome, suggesting [that* korbanos *are only meant to be] a demonstration against wicked and foolish individuals, while the Torah says that* korbanos *are* the food of the fire, for a satisfying aroma *(3:16).*

*Besides, [*korbanos*] would not cure the Egyptians of their foolish beliefs. On the contrary, it would reinforce* *their mindset. The Egyptians worship the constellations of Aries the Ram, and Taurus the Bull, thinking these constellations wield power [over their lives.] They do not eat the meat of sheep and cattle out of respect for the power and influence exerted by these animals. If so, slaughtering these animals for the holy Name of Hashem, is an honor and a tribute to [these constellations.] In fact, idol worshippers themselves used to do that, as it says,* [Bnei Yisrael] will then stop sacrificing to the goat-demons after whom they stray *(17:7), and we find that the people who made the eigel sacrificed to [the calf]. The Rambam himself writes that idol worshippers sacrificed to the moon at the beginning of the month and to the sun when it entered certain constellations. The disease of idolatry would have been cured more effectively if we ate our fill of the cattle and sheep [they worshiped], for in their eyes, this would be a revolting transgression, something they would never do!*

Furthermore, when Noach and his three sons left the ark, there were no Chaldeans or Egyptians in the world, yet Noach offered a korban *which pleased Hashem, as it says,* Hashem smelled the appeasing fragrance, and because of it, He said to Himself, "Never again will I curse the soil because of man" (Bereishis *8:21).*

It also says, Hevel too, offered some of the firstborn of his flock, from the fattest ones. Hashem paid heed to Hevel and his offering (4:4), in spite of the fact that no idol worship existed in the world at that time! (Malachi 1:12)

Additionally Bilam said, "I have set up seven altars, and I have sacrificed a bull and ram as a burnt offering on each altar" (Bamidbar *23:4). [Bilam] did not [bring sacrifices] to oppose the folly of idol worship, and he was not commanded to [bring the offerings]. He did it in order to come close to G-d, so He would speak to him.*

The Torah describes korbanos *in terms of,* My offering, My food for My fires, My satisfying aroma (Bamidbar *28:2). Heaven forbid that they should have no purpose and significance other than opposing the folly of idol worship.*

The Rabbis' reason for the korbanos *makes much more sense: Man's plans are realized through thought, speech, and action. Therefore, Hashem commanded that a person who committed a sin bring a* korban. *Leaning his hands on the* korban, *atones for his actions; verbally confessing his sin, atones for the speech which brought about the sin; burning the innards and kidneys which are the instruments of man's thought and desire atones for his thoughts; burning the legs of the korban atones because his hands and feet do all his work; dashing the blood of the* korban *on the altar corresponds to his soul which resides in his blood. When he does these things, the sinner is mindful that he sinned against G–d with his body and soul. He realizes that his blood should be spilled and his body burned, were it not for the kindness of the Creator, Who accepts a substitute from him. His* korban *atones for him; its blood atones for his blood, its life force atones for his soul, and the limbs of the* korban *atones for his limbs. Portions [are given to the kohanim] supporting the teachers of the Torah so that they pray for him.*

The regular daily korbanos *are brought because the entire community cannot possibly avoid transgressing all the time. This explanation makes sense and inspires the heart as Aggadic teachings do.*

Chapter Thirty-three

Teaching Moderation

The Torah also aims to restrain a person, making him control his desires, curb his appetites and indulge only when necessary.

People can be intemperate with food, drink and sexual intercourse. This can ruin a person, disrupting harmony in a family and community, because a person who is obsessed with lust cannot think straight. He inflicts harm on his body, shortening his life because his worries increase as envy, hatred, and claims about stolen property abound. Because a fool pursues pleasure for its own sake, Hashem gave us mitzvos to eradicate this mental outlook, diverting our thoughts from immorality and preventing us from giving in to excessive desire and lust.

Thus the Torah commanded us to kill the wayward and rebellious son, who will stop at nothing to satisfy his obsession with food and drink. He is characterized as *a glutton and a drunkard* (*Devarim* 21:20). The Torah commands us to stone him, eliminating him before he corrupts decent youngsters.

Complacency and Acceptance

The Torah fosters the quality of refinement and politeness. A person should be understanding, calm, and tranquil, rather than stubborn and arrogant. Therefore, we have the following commandments: *Remove the barriers from your heart, and do not remain so stubborn any more* (*Devarim* 10:16); *Pay attention and listen Yisrael* (ibid. 27:9); *If you are willing and obey* (*Yeshayah* 1:10). Yisrael accepted these mitzvos in the following verses: *When we hear it we will do it* (*Devarim* 5:24), or in a metaphorical way, *Draw me; we will run after You* (*Shir Hashirim* 1:4).

HOLINESS AND PURITY

Additionally, the Torah wishes to instill purity and holiness in the Jewish people, which is achieved by restraining from frequent sexual intercourse, as I will explain.

When G-d commanded Moshe to sanctify the people in order to receive the Torah, He said, *Sanctify them today and tomorrow* (*Shemos* 19:10). Moshe said, *Do not come near your wives* (ibid. v.15), hinting that holiness means abstaining from sexual intercourse. Similarly, abstaining from wine is called holiness, for it says about a *nazir*, *He shall be holy* (*Bamidbar* 6:5).

According to *Sifra*, the passage, *You must make yourselves holy and remain sanctified* (*Vayikra* 11:44), refers to the holiness that doing the mitzvos brings. Just as the Torah calls fulfillment of the mitzvos holiness and purity, so it calls the transgression of them defilement, as I will explain.

The Torah mandates clean clothing and bathing to remove dirt and perspiration, but this must go hand in hand with purity of action and a heart free of flawed beliefs and immoral character traits.

It is contemptible to be satisfied with the external purity obtained by bathing and laundering clothing, while luxuriating in food and lust. Yeshayah describes such people, saying, *Those who prepare and purify themselves to go to the gardens, going one group after another to its midst, and those who eat the flesh of swine, worms and mice* (*Yeshayah* 66:17). He refers to people who purify themselves outwardly for all to see, but who engage in sinful behavior, eating swine's flesh, worms and mice, in the privacy of their room. The phrase, *going one group after another to its midst*, may allude to forbidden sexual intercourse.

The prophet tells us: [These people] appear clean on the surface, but in their heart they harbor lust and lewdness. This is not what the Torah has in mind. Its main purpose is to teach us restraint, urging people to cleanse their outward appearance only after purifying their heart. Those who bathe their bodies and launder their garments while remaining soiled by their actions and bad character traits are described by Shelomoh as, *A generation that is pure in its own eyes and does not cleanse itself of filth, whose eyes are very haughty and whose eyelids are arched* (*Mishlei* 30:12,13).

The ideas mentioned in this chapter should help you discover the reasons for many mitzvos you did not previously comprehend.

Chapter Thirty-four

Extraordinary Circumstances

The Torah and mitzvos do not deal with individual cases or extraordinary circumstances. Its goals, whether in the ideological, moral, or practical realm, are geared to general conditions, not making exceptions for harm that might be caused to a single individual through a Torah decree.

There are forces in nature that benefit mankind as a whole, yet may harm individual persons.[9] Likewise, we cannot be surprised when the Torah, which comes from Hashem as natural forces do, does not bring equal levels of [spiritual perfection] to everyone. Some people will not attain perfection by fulfilling certain mitzvos, just as in nature there are creatures whose needs are not met by specific natural events. For all this comes from one G-d, is the work of one Creator, *coming from one Shepherd* (*Koheles* 12:11). It is impossible [that the needs of every creature can be met through nature,] and we have already explained that since it is impossible not to have exceptions there will surely be exceptions. The mitzvos cannot, like medicine, change according to the different conditions of persons and times. While a medication is adapted to the patient's current condition, the Torah must be absolute and universal. If the Torah were modified according to individual needs, it would be imperfect; the mitzvos would be variable. The fundamental principles of the Torah cannot be dependent on a certain time or place. On the contrary; the laws must be definitive, clear-cut, and universal, as G-d said, *There shall be one Torah and one law for you and for the proselyte* (*Bamidbar* 15:15). As mentioned before, the mitzvos are intended to benefit the majority.

With this introduction, I will explain [the reasons for the mitzvos].

---

9 For example: Rainfall is beneficial to farmers but unwelcome for construction workers.

Chapter Thirty-five

The Fourteen Classes of the Law

I have divided all mitzvos into fourteen classes.[10]

The first class includes the mitzvos that are fundamental beliefs, such as the mitzvos listed [in *Mishneh Torah*] as "Laws of Fundamental Principles of the Torah." The mitzvos of *teshuvah* and fasts are also included in this class.

The second class contains the mitzvos connected with the prohibition of idolatry, described [in *Mishneh Torah*] as "Laws of Idolatry." The laws about *shaatneiz*—garments made of linen combined with wool, *orlah*—fruit from trees in their first three years, and *kilayim*—diverse seeds in a vineyard—are also contained in this class since these mitzvos were intended to establish basic beliefs in people's minds.

Mitzvos in the third class improve moral and ethical character traits. They are listed in [*Mishneh Torah*] under the title "Laws of Character Traits." Refined character traits help people function together, which is essential for society.

Tzedakah, loans, gifts, and the like are part of the fourth class of mitzvos. These include the laws of vows of valuation and consecration, laws dealing with loans and servants, and all the laws listed in the Book of Agriculture, except for *kilayim* and *orlah* which we already said are included in the second class. These mitzvos benefit everyone at one point in time or another. For although one may be

[10] The Rambam's monumental code of all the mitzvos, Mishneh Torah, is also called Yad Hachazakah. The word *yad* numerically equals fourteen (yud (10), and dalet (4) = 14) alluding to the fourteen books of the code. The fourteen classes of mitzvos basically conform to the fourteen books.

rich today, he or his descendants may be poor tomorrow; and vice-versa.

The fifth class comprises the mitzvos preventing wrongdoing and violence. They are included in [*Mishneh Torah*] in the section of "Damages." Their benefit is obvious.

The sixth is the class of laws concerning penalties, such as the laws of theft, robbery, and false witnesses. Most of the laws contained in the section of "Judges" [in *Mishneh Torah*] belong to this class. The benefit [of these laws] is also obvious, for if an offender is not punished there would be no end to damage and crime, nor would wrongdoers be deterred. Abrogating fines and penalties is not merciful; on the contrary it would be the height of cruelty, destroying the social fabric of the country. It is with compassion that Hashem commanded, *Appoint yourself judges and police in all your settlements* (*Devarim* 16:18).

The seventh class regulates financial transactions between individuals, with loans, hire for wages, deposits, buying and selling and the like included. Rules about inheritance also belong to this class. These laws are described in the sections of "Acquisitions and Judgments" [in *Mishneh Torah*.] The purpose of these laws is clear, for people everywhere engage in financial dealings, and fair and impartial laws are necessary to regulate these transactions.

The laws of Shabbos and Yamim Tovim, when work is forbidden, comprise the eighth class of mitzvos, which are discussed in the section of "Times" [in *Mishneh Torah*]. The Torah explicitly states that the purpose of these mitzvos is to impart an ideology or provide physical relaxation.

The ninth class encompasses the elements of daily worship services, such as prayer, reciting the *Shemah*, etc., listed in the section of "Love" [in *Mishneh Torah*]. The mitzvah of *milah*, though it is listed there, is not included. These laws strengthen our love of G–d, reinforcing our belief in Him and His attributes.

The tenth class covers the mitzvos relating to the Sanctuary, its utensils, and those who perform its services. They are listed in the section of "Service" [in *Mishneh Torah*]. We have mentioned the reason for these mitzvos [in chapter 32].

The eleventh class includes the laws of sacrifices, which are in the sections of "Service" and "Sacrifices" [in *Mishneh Torah*]. We have already explained [in chapter 32] why sacrifices were needed at the time [of the Giving of the Torah] and the benefit of those laws.

The twelfth class contains the laws dealing with things unclean and clean. These laws discouraged people from entering the Beis Hamikdash [too frequently], enabling them to be overwhelmed with awe and reverence when they did approach the Beis Hamikdash.

The thirteenth class embraces the laws of forbidden foods and related issues. They are listed [in *Mishneh Torah*] under the titles of "Forbidden Foods" and "Laws of Slaughtering." The mitzvos dealing with vows and *nazir* also belong in this class. The purpose of these laws is to mitigate the desire for physical gratification, [so no one will] think food and drink are the source of ultimate bliss. We expounded on this in our introduction to *Pirkei Avos*.

The fourteenth class, covering the laws of forbidden sexual intercourse, is listed under the laws of "Forbidden Sexual Intercourse" [in *Mishneh Torah*]. Laws about interbreeding of livestock also belong in this category. These laws, like the ones in the previous class, restrain man from indulgence, underscoring that lust is not the purpose of man's existence as the savage pagans believe. The laws of *milah* are also included in this class.

All mitzvos are categorized either as mitzvos between man and G-d or mitzvos between man and his fellow man. The fifth, sixth, seventh and part of the third classes deal with mitzvos between man and his fellow man. The rest deal with mitzvos between man and G-d, meaning they teach good character traits and beliefs which benefit the individual who performs them. Although these mitzvos eventually will help in his relationship with others, this will be only indirectly, whereas the mitzvos between man and his fellow man affect his fellow directly.

With this outline in place, I will explain the purpose of those mitzvos that seem useless or unfathomable, except for a few whose purpose I do not yet understand.

Chapter Thirty-six

Fundamental Principles

There is an obvious reason for the mitzvos listed [in *Mishneh Torah*] as Fundamental Principals of the Torah. Examining each one, you will clearly see its message. Likewise, the reason for having mitzvos that urge us to learn and teach are obvious, for without knowledge one cannot do good deeds nor have the proper outlook on life.

Certainly, we should honor the teachers of the Torah, which leads people to respect them and accept their teachings about what to believe and what to do. This mitzvah includes the requirement to be humble, as it says, *Stand up before a white head* (*Vayikra* 19:32). The mitzvah to swear by G-d's name and the prohibition of swearing falsely or in vain are also included because these mitzvos glorify G-d, promoting belief in His greatness. Likewise, the mitzvah to cry out to G-d in time of trouble, and *to blow an alarm with the trumpets* (*Bamidbar* 10:9), belongs to this class, since this is an expression of true belief, demonstrating that we believe G-d is aware of our circumstances and He can make us successful if we obey Him or ruin us if we disobey Him. That [fortune and misfortune] do not come about by chance is expressed in the verse, *If you treat My acts as accident* (*Vayikra* 26:21) meaning:, If I punish you with troubles which you consider to be only bad luck, I will punish you even more gravely and harshly. This is what is meant by the passage, *If you still treat My acts as chance, then I will treat you with a vengeance of chance* (ibid. v. 27,28). If people believe their troubles are flukes of nature they will continue in their false beliefs without repenting from their evil way of life, as it says, *You have stricken them but they have not felt sickened* (*Yirmeyah* 5:3).

Therefore, G-d commanded us to be submissive to Him, praying and crying out to Him in time of trouble.

Teshuvah

Of course repentance belongs in this class because it is an essential principle of faith for a Jew who believes in the Torah. No man is absolutely free of sin; he may err because he does not know the mitzvos he has to follow, or he may fall prey to lust or anger. If he would believe there was no remedy for his transgressions he would forever continue transgressing, perhaps even adding other sins to them, since he sees no way out for himself. But with *teshuvah* he can correct himself, returning to a better way and becoming even more perfect than he was before he sinned.

There are many mitzvos that confirm the concept of teshuvah, including confession, sacrifices for unintentional sins and for some intentional sins, and fasts. These mitzvos are clearly beneficial; like teshuvah, their goal is to help you repent from the sins you committed, and resolve to stop sinning.

Chapter Thirty-seven

The Laws of Idolatry

The mitzvos listed [in *Mishneh Torah*] under Laws of Idolatry, save people from the error of idolatry and the evil practices associated with it, such as divining auspicious times, divining by omens, practicing witchcraft, using incantations, and the like. Witchcraft was part of the rituals of the Sabeans, Kasdim, and Chaldeans, and even more so of the Egyptians and Canaanites. They convinced others—as they themselves were convinced—that these acts of sorcery gave them power to perform spectacular things for an individual or for the inhabitants of a city, despite the fact that none of the witches ever achieved results, nor did it make intellectual sense to, for example, gather certain plants at a certain time, or take a specific number of a certain object.

Witchcraft

Witchcraft comprised three kinds of practices: Those involving natural objects such as plants, animals, and minerals; the witchcraft linked to a certain time; and thirdly, witchcraft involving human action, such as dancing, clapping hands, shouting, laughing, jumping with one leg, laying on the ground, burning something, fumigating certain kinds of incense, speaking words, or uttering gibberish.

Sometimes, all three types of witchcraft were practiced together. For example, a witch might say, "Take a leaf of this plant when the moon is under this sign of the zodiac in the east. Also, take some of the horn, sweat, hair, and blood of this animal when the sun is in the middle of the sky. Melt this metal at this conjunction of the sun and moon and position of the stars. Then, speak certain words and fumigate these leaves to the molten image, and such and such a thing will happen."

In some cases one of the procedures was enough. In most cases, women were required to perform these actions. Thus, for rain-making, ten virgins, adorned with jewelry and wearing red dresses, would dance, jumping forward and backward, making gestures to the sun, and performing a lengthy operation until, as they believed, rain would come pouring down. Additionally, if four women lay on their backs with their feet spread apart and lifted up, while saying certain words and doing certain things in this shameful position, hail would stop coming down in that place. There are many such senseless stories, with women always performing the witchcraft.

Witchcraft and Astrology

Witchcraft is closely associated with astrology. Witchcraft practitioners imagine that every plant, animal, or mineral is assigned to a certain star. Witchcraft is a form of worship of that star, which fulfills their wishes after being pleased with the acts, words, or offerings of incense.

The purpose of the Torah is to uproot idolatry completely, obliterating the idea that any star could harm or help a person, because this leads to the worship of stars. It was necessary to eliminate all witches since they were all idol worshipers, though their worship was peculiar, differing from the conventional worship of these deities. Since most of these forms of witchcraft require women to officiate, the Torah says, *Do not allow a sorceress to live* (*Shemos* 22:17). Another reason the Torah specifies women is because people naturally feel pity when a woman is executed. Similarly, with these verses concerning idolatry, *When you discover a man or woman doing evil* (*Devarim* 17:2), and *You shall pelt the man or woman to death with stones* (ibid. v.5) the Torah specifies the punishment of women, which is not done for desecrating the Shabbos or any other law. This is because people have an innate feeling of pity for women.

Words of the Covenant

In the "Words of the Covenant" (*Devarim* 28:69), the Torah warns that the very misfortunes you think idolatry and witchcraft will prevent, will, in fact, befall you [if you worship idols.] Since witches believed their witchcraft drove away dangerous animals; protected vegetation from various kinds of damage; killed worms that infest vineyards; and manipulated nature to prevent hail from coming down, and leaves and fruit from dropping off trees, the Torah explicitly states, *I will send wild beasts among you, killing your children* (*Vayikra* 26:22), and, *I will send against them fanged beast with venomous creatures that crawl* (*Devarim* 32:24), and, *All your trees and the fruit of the land will be reduced by the crickets* (ibid. 28:42), and, *You will plant vineyards and work hard, but the worms will eat the grapes. You will have olive trees in all your territories, but the olives will drop off and you will not enjoy their oil* (ibid. v.39,40).

Though idolaters tried to convince people that idolatry prevents misfortune and brings benefit, actually the opposite is true. Idol worship prevents one from reaping any benefit and causes misfortune, as it says in the "Words of the Covenant." The Torah specifies these curses and blessings, so we can infer the great benefit [of refraining from idol worship.]

Ways of the Amorites

To keep away from witchcraft we are forbidden to adopt any practice of the idolaters, even those that relate to farming, cattle-breeding, and similar occupations. [The Torah] prohibits any irrational act the idolaters thought was effective through witchcraft, as it says, *Do not follow the customs of the nations that I am driving out before you* (*Vayikra* 18:3). The Sages call such acts "ways of the Amorites." They are kinds of witchcraft, since they are irrational and akin to witchcraft which is based on astrology. Thus, "the ways of the Amorites" lead people to extolling, worshiping, and praising the stars.

Our Sages said: Anything used as medicine is exempt from the law of "the ways of the Amorites," meaning cures based on natural processes are permitted. However, irrational cures are prohibited. Therefore, if someone said, "A tree whose fruits fall off may be loaded with stones or dyed red," the following objection was raised: Loading the tree with stones may be justified on the grounds that it reduces its sap, but why should one be permitted to dye the tree red? Dyeing a tree red and similar things that do not make sense, are prohibited as "ways of the Amorites." For the same reason our Sages said: The placenta of an animal that was consecrated for the Sanctuary must be buried. It may not be hung from a tree or buried at a cross-road, because this is one of the "ways of the Amorites." From this precedent we learn how to deal with similar cases.

It is permitted to use a nail of the gallows and the tooth of a fox as a remedy because these cures were established by research in those days, and considered empirical facts. They were helpful, just as hanging a peony over a person suffering from epileptic seizures, or applying a dog's excrements to a sore throat, or applying the vapors of vinegar and marcasite[11] to swollen tendons were efficacious cures. It is permitted to use any remedy that experience has shown to be effective even if it does not stand to reason. The above-named cures are permitted just as [the standard remedy of] taking laxatives for stomach trouble [is permitted].

Dear reader, learn these things, *for they are a graceful wreath upon your head, a necklace around your throat* (*Mishlei* 1:9).

---

[11] A mineral with crystal structure

Idolatrous Customs

As we explained in *Mishneh Torah,* it is forbidden to shave the corners of the head and the corners of the beard, since that was the custom of the idolatrous priests. For the same reason, wearing *shaatneiz*—garments made of linen and wool, is forbidden. As is recorded in their books, the pagan priests adorned themselves with garments containing vegetable and animal material while holding a ring made of a mineral in their hand. The prohibition, *No male clothing shall be on a woman, and a man shall not wear a woman's garment* (*Devarim* 22:5) is similarly derived; the book Tumtum records that men wore women's clothing when standing [in prayer] before the planet Venus, and women carried a shield and weapons when standing before Mars. I think switching attire is also prohibited because it arouses lust, leading to immorality.

Abolition of Pagan Beliefs

It is forbidden to derive any benefit from idolatry, because it becomes a stumbling block for a person. A person may buy an idol intending to shatter it, but is convinced to keep it. Even if he melts it and sells [the metal] to an idolater, he is forbidden to use the money he receives, because people will mistake an incidental matter for the decisive factor in their life. For example, a successful person may attribute his good luck to living in a certain house, or owning a certain animal or article. Likewise, if the person profits from the money he received for the [melted] idol, he may attribute his success to the idol. He would then trust in the idol, which contravenes everything the Torah stands for, as is clearly spelled out in numerous verses.

Therefore, we are forbidden to benefit from the coverings of idols, their offerings, and their vessels, protecting ourselves from [ascribing our fortune to idols]. Because star worship was very strong in those days, with people believing that the stars controlled life and death, and brought good and bad luck, the Torah uses strong measures such as covenants, witnesses, and the above-mentioned curses to expunge this ideology, and forbids deriving benefit from any part of an idol. Indeed, in the verse *Do not bring any abominable [idol] into your house, since you may become [repulsive] like it* (*Devarim* 7:26), G-d warns us that if money received for an idol is mixed with someone's property, He will obliterate that property. The laws relating to idolatry are meant to end this harmful creed and keep us away from it.

Giving Children to Molech

People who wish to promote baseless doctrines often use scurrilous tactics to spread their faith, predicting that such-and-such disease will strike if someone doesn't do a specific religious action. A person may catch this illness some day and think that it happened because he did not do that symbolic act, causing him to adopt idolatry.

A person's greatest fear is the loss of his property and children. With that in mind, the ancient worshipers of fire spread the hoax that if one did not pass his son or daughter over fire, the child would die. Despite its absurdity, people rushed to do this, fearing for their children's lives, especially since passing a child over a fire is a trifling thing to do.

Because women, who have an emotional nature, care for young children, this practice was especially prevalent. The Torah strongly opposed this practice, using stronger language than for any other idolatrous worship, saying, *I will direct My anger against that person . . . since he has given his child to Molech, thus defiling that which is holy to Me, and profaning My holy name* (*Vayikra* 20:2). The true prophet [Moshe] declares in the name of G-d that the very act which is performed to keep the child alive will bring death upon the one who performs it and destruction on his offspring, saying, *I will direct My anger against this person and his family* (ibid. 20:5).

Remnants of this practice have survived even to the present time because of its popularity, with some midwives placing foul-smelling incense in fire and then swinging small babies wrapped in blankets through the smoke rising from the fire. This is absolutely forbidden. Despite the Torah's opposition over thousands of years, the remnants of this worship have not been wiped out, pointing to the shrewdness of this religion's founder.

Forbidden Fruit

Just as they cautioned that any child not passed through the fire would die, idolaters decreed that the *asheirah* tree should be worshiped, with one part of its fruit offered as a sacrifice and the remainder eaten in the idol's temple. They warned that without this service the tree would dry up, with its fruits falling off and its harvest dwindling or the tree might be stricken by some other disease. Since people were afraid of losing their money, they rushed to offer their first-fruit to the *asheirah*. Therefore the Torah commands us to burn the first three years of produce of fruit-trees, promising that the destruction of this fruit will be followed by years of plenty of fruit, as it says, *In the fifth year you may eat its fruit and thus increase your crops* (*Vayikra* 19:25). We are commanded to eat the fruit of the fourth year before G-d [in Yerushalayim], as opposed [to the pagan custom] of eating *orlah*—the fruit of the first three years—in the temples of the idols, as we have described.

According to the Nabatean Agriculture, the ancient idolaters caused certain substances to decay, and after waiting for the sun to stand in a certain position relative to the zodiac they performed many acts of witchcraft with this [decomposed] substance. They said that spreading some of this matter around or under a tree works like a charm, making it grow faster and produce more fruit.

For this reason, the Torah forbids us to use the fruit of a tree during its first three years, to obviate any opportunity to accelerate the harvest of any tree. After three years, most fruit trees in Eretz Yisrael bear fruit through natural growth without the black magic commonly practiced in those days.

Grafting Trees

Another belief of the Sabeans was that grafting one tree onto another when the sun and the moon were in a specific position, while fumigating it with a certain herb and reciting an incantation, will benefit the tree. There was another ceremony to graft an olive tree on an esrog tree. I believe the book of medicines stored away by Chizkiyah spoke of this. The Sabeans added that the grafting must be done by a maiden while a man has unnatural sexual relations with her. This practice was common because the pleasure of the sexual intercourse combined with the excitement of the anticipated benefits of the grafting.

Because we must shun the ways of the idolaters and their abominations, the Torah prohibits grafting one tree onto another. As a corollary to the prohibition of grafting trees, we are forbidden to sow two kinds of seeds together or close to each other. Therefore you will find that grafting [which is forbidden because of idolatry] is totally prohibited and is punishable by forty lashes, however, sowing different seeds near each other is only forbidden in Eretz Yisrael. . . .

Thus, the prohibitions of wearing a garment of wool combined with linen, or using fruit of a tree that grew in the first three years, and mixing diverse species are connected to idolatry; and the prohibition against adopting the "ways of the Amorites" is to eradicate anything leading to idolatry.

CHAPTER THIRTY-EIGHT

ACQUIRING MORAL QUALITIES

The third class of mitzvos recorded in *Hilchos Dei'os,* Laws of Character Traits, [such as emulating G-d's ways, to love converts, to avoid embarrassing others, to shun gossip, not to hold a grudge, etc.] are rules of moral conduct to guide interpersonal relations. Their purpose is clear enough, and needs no elaboration.

Some mitzvos although they require specific action and people consider them Torah decrees which have no purpose, they are nevertheless intended to instill a constructive moral trait, as we will explain each one in its proper place. However, the goal of the mitzvos mentioned in *Hilchos Dei'os* is clearly to train people to acquire good character traits.

Chapter Thirty-nine

Charity and Compassion

We were commanded the mitzvos in the section of Agriculture of *Mishneh Torah* to instill compassion for the poor and downtrodden in us, to help the needy in a variety of ways, to avoid hurting the feelings of those in need, and not to anger those who are despondent. The mitzvos about portions to be given to the poor are also self-understood.

Gifts for Kohen and Levi

The reason for the mitzvos of *terumah* and *maaseir*[12] is stated in the Torah, *For [the Levi] does not have a hereditary portion with you* (*Devarim* 14:29). The Levi'im did not have a share [in the Land] so the whole tribe could devote themselves exclusively to the service of G-d and the study of the Torah. Rather than plowing or harvesting, they focused on serving G-d, as it says, *They shall teach Your law to Yaakov and Your Torah to Yisrael* (*Devarim* 33:10). The Torah often juxtaposes the Levi next to the convert, the orphan, and the widow; because a Levi was considered a poor man since he did not own property.

The Second Tithe

Maaseir sheini, the second tithe, was spent on food to be eaten in Yerushalayim, thus the farmer would certainly give part of this tithe as charity. Since he must spend the tithe on food and

12 The offerings given to the kohen and the Levi.

drink, it was easy to give some of it away, bit by bit. This mitzvah caused a multitude of people to converge on Yerushalayim which strengthened the bond of brotherly love among the Jewish people.

GIFTS OF "FIRSTS"

The law about the fruit of the tree in its fourth year is related to idolatrous customs as we stated [in chapter 38]. But it also has another purpose, similar to the purpose for offering the kohanim the gifts of *challah,*[13] *bikkurim,*[14] and the first of the shearing. The first of everything must be dedicated to G-d, thus accustoming a person to generosity, helping him to curb his desire for riches. That is why the Kohen received the cheek, the right shoulder and the stomach of animals, because the cheek is the beginning of the animal, the right shoulder is the first of the extremities, and the stomach is the first of the inner organs.

THE BIKKURIM DECLARATION

The one who carries the basket of *bikkurim*—first fruits—on his shoulder, bringing them to the kohen, recites verses that inspire him to be humble, since this declaration proclaims the kindness and goodness of Hashem.[15]

This affirmation teaches him to remember the times of trouble in days of contentment. The Torah repeats this theme many times, as in, *You must remember that you were slaves in Egypt* (*Devarim* 5:16). For people raised in wealth and comfort may adopt the vices of conceit and arrogance, abandoning the true belief, as it says, *You may then eat and be satisfied, building fine houses and living in them. Your herds and flocks may increase, and you may amass much*

[13] The first portion of every dough was given to the kohen.

[14] The first fruits grown in Eretz Yisrael were given to the kohen.

[15] *Devarim* 26:3-10 relates that when one brings *bikkurim* to the kohen he makes a declaration acknowledging Hashem's kindness starting from before the exodus from Egypt and including inheriting the land of Israel and growing this crop.

silver and gold—everything you own may increase. But your heart may then grow haughty, and you may forget Hashem your G-d, the One that brought you out of the slave house that was Egypt (ibid. 8:12-14), and, *Yeshurun thus became fat and rebelled* (ibid. 32:15). Therefore, the Torah commanded us to read the *bikkurim* declaration each year when the first fruits are brought to the *Beis Hamikdash*, the dwelling place of the *Shechinah*.

The Torah emphasizes that we always remember the plagues of the Egyptians, as it says, *So that you will remember the day you left Egypt all the days of your life* (ibid. 16:3), and, *So that you will be able to tell you children and grandchildren how I made fools of the Egyptians* (*Shemos* 10:2). These events illustrate the truth of prophecy, reward, and punishment. We all recognize the benefit of mitzvos that preserve the memory of miracles or instill the [true] faith.

Sanctity of the First Born

The reason for the mitzvah of [redeeming] the first-born of man and cattle is given in the following verse. *When Pharaoh stubbornly refused to let us go, Hashem killed all the first-born in Egypt, man and beast alike. I therefore sacrifice to Hashem all male firstling [animals] and redeem all first-born of my sons* (*Shemos* 8:15). Only cattle, sheep, and donkeys are mentioned in this mitzvah, since these are domestic animals and easily available, especially in Eretz Yisrael where the Jews were shepherds, as it says, *We are shepherds, we and our fathers before us* (*Bereishis* 37:3). Because shepherds usually don't keep horses and camels [they are not mentioned]. Only oxen, sheep, and donkeys are mentioned by the spoils of Midian (*Bamidbar* ch.31), because farmers and lumbermen need them. Yaakov also said, *I have acquired cattle, donkeys, and sheep* (*Bereishis* 31:6). Camels and horses were kept only sporadically. The commandment to break the neck of the first-born of a donkey [if it was not redeemed] guarantees the redemption of the donkey. Therefore, the Mishnah says that the mitzvah of redeeming the donkey is preferable to breaking its neck.

Shemittah and Yovel

The mitzvos of *shemittah* and *yovel*—the sabbatical year and the jubilee[16]—promote the qualities of compassion and benevolence, as the Torah says *The needy among you will then be able to eat [from your field] just as you do, and whatever is left over can be eaten by wild animals* (*Shemos* 23:11). Furthermore, soil improves and produce increases if the land is left fallow. Other mitzvos [of shemittah and yovel] foster kindness to slaves and the indigent by cancelling all claims to debts and freeing all slaves [in the *yovel* year]. Some of these mitzvos provide a lasting source of sustenance by ensuring that the land remains the enduring property of its owners, since it could not be sold permanently, as it says, *The land shall not be sold in perpetuity* (*Vayikra* 25:23). Thus, a person was able to keep his property for himself and his heirs, to enjoy its produce. These are the reasons for the mitzvos listed in the section of Agriculture of *Mishneh Torah.*

Treatment of Slaves

The mitzvos about slaves recorded in *Mishneh Torah,* caution us to perform acts of mercy and kindness to the helpless. It is merciful [to force a master] to free his slave for the loss of a limb,[17] [since this will restrain the master from mutilating his slave], and [the slave] will not suffer a double indignity, from slavery and from the disability. This applies even when the slave's tooth has been knocked out, and certainly if other parts of the body have been mangled. The slave may only be punished with a rod or reed and the like. Additionally, if a master strikes his slave too hard and kills him, he is punished with death; it is considered murder. Another

---

16 During the shemittah and yovel years the fields could not be planted and all the produce could be eaten by anyone. All debts were cancelled. In the yovel year all land reverted to its original owner and all Jewish slaves were freed.

17 *Shemos* 21:26,27 relates that if a master maimed a limb of his slave the slave is set free.

mitzvah involving pity is, *If a slave seeks refuge with you from his master, you must not turn him back over to his master* (*Devarim* 23:16).

This mitzvah also teaches us to adopt the wonderful trait of offering shelter to those who ask for our protection, rather than handing them over to their pursuers. Not only must we protect them, we must actively care for them, and refrain from paining them with hateful words. And so the Torah says, *[The runaway slave] must be allowed to live alongside you wherever he chooses in your settlements. You must do nothing to hurt his feelings* (ibid. v.17). If we must treat the lowliest of men, the slave, this way, certainly we must help a respectable person who is in need of our assistance.

No Mercy For the Wicked

On the other hand, if a sinner or wicked man seeks our protection we must not grant it, nor show him any mercy. His punishment may not be mitigated even if he appeals to the most revered person for leniency, as it says [about a murderer,] *One must even take him from My altar to put him to death* (*Shemos* 21:14). For example, [Yoav] sought G-d's protection [from his pursuers] by taking hold of the horns of the altar. But [Shelomoh] did not grant it (1 *Melachim* 2:28-34). He ordered [Yoav] to be turned over to the court from which he had escaped. Surely had [Yoav] sought the protection of an ordinary person, he would not have been helped, for showing mercy to sinners is cruelty to all people.

The Torah describes these moral qualities as *righteous rules and laws* (*Devarim* 4:8), in sharp contrast to pagan morality which considers a person praiseworthy when he helps his fellowman, regardless of whether the asylum-seeker is the oppressor or the oppressed.[18] This is evident by the way they glorify the indiscriminate offering of hospitality in their legends and ballads. We have explained the reason for every mitzvah in this section.

---

[18] Arabs extol the quality of offering hospitality to whomever asks for it, even the most despicable criminal.

Chapter Forty

Damage and Injury

The mitzvos of the fifth category found in the section of Damages in *Mishneh Torah,* focus on removing injustice and preventing injury. The Torah holds us liable for any injury caused by our property or our action, if we could have prevented it, so we will be very careful to avoid damaging something. Because we are responsible for any damage caused by our cattle, we will guard them. We are similarly liable for [damage caused by] fire and pits; because they are manmade, the builder is responsible to make sure they don't cause damage. These laws are fair as we will show.

Damage Caused by One's Animals

One need not pay for the damage caused by the tooth and foot of an animal [i.e., what the animal eats and the damage it causes in the course of walking] in a public place, because one cannot take precautions against that, and the damage caused is insignificant. People who place their things in a public place are exposing themselves to harm and placing their property at risk. But compensation for damage caused by the tooth or foot of an animal in a private field must be paid to the owner of the property.

However, damage caused by the horn of animals has a different status. Because precautions can be taken so the animal should not cause injury anywhere, and in a public thoroughfare a person cannot always guard his possessions against accidents of this kind, the law is the same for [private and public] places. But the law does differentiate between an owner who has been warned about his animal, and one who did not know his animal was dangerous. If the animal was not known to gore, the owner must pay only half the damage, but damage caused by an animal that is known to habitually gore must be paid in full. . . .

Killing a Pursuer

These mitzvos include the commandment to kill a man who pursues another person if he chases him with the intent to murder him or to commit a sexual offense. In only these two instances may we prevent a person from committing a crime by killing him, since in both those cases, the damage cannot be rectified.

If someone had intention to transgress a commandment that is punishable by the death penalty of the human court, such as idolatry and the desecration of Shabbos, but he did not actually commit the sin, nor has he harmed another person, he is not put to death.

Desire is frowned upon because it leads to craving, and craving is forbidden because it leads to robbery, as our Sages have stated.

Returning Lost Property

It is easy to understand the reason for the mitzvah of returning lost property (*Devarim* 22:1-30). It is an excellent way of furthering friendly relations between people, and its benefit is reciprocal. If you won't return your neighbor's lost property, he won't return your lost property to you, just as your son won't honor you if you don't honor your father. There are many other such examples.

The Accidental Murderer

A person who killed someone unintentionally must go into exile because the anger of the blood avenger cools down when the perpetrator is out of sight. [The accidental murderer] returns home upon the death of the most revered and beloved person in Yisrael, [the *Kohen Gadol*]. The relative of the slain victim will be soothed by [the *Kohen Gadol's*] death, for it is human nature to find consolation when the same or a greater misfortune happens to another person. And no death is more painful for us than the death of the *Kohen Gadol*.

The Eglah Arufah

The mitzvah of the *eglah arufah*,[19] "the axed calf," is clearly beneficial, for the city nearest to the murder victim must bring the calf, and very likely the murderer lives there. According to the Sages, the elders of that city call on G-d to be their witness that they have kept the roads in good condition and provided protection for passing travelers, and that they do not know who killed this person. Many times, because of the tumult of the investigation, when the elders walk [out of the city] and bring the calf, people begin talking, and the murderer may be identified through the publicity. Or perhaps through a clue someone figures out who the murderer is. If anyone, whether man, woman, or handmaid, identifies a person as the murderer, the calf is not killed.

It is deplorable for someone to withhold information about the killer while the elders ask G-d to be their witness that they know nothing about the killer. Therefore, even a woman will come forth to testify if she knows who the murderer is. It serves a purpose to find the murderer because even if the court cannot sentence him to

---

[19] *Devarim* 21:1-8 relates that if a corpse is found slain outside a city, the elders of the city take a calf and break its neck at a stream. They declare their innocence, further stating that they do not know the killer.

death, the king, who has the power to impose the death sentence on the basis of circumstantial evidence, may find him guilty. And if the king does not kill him, the blood avenger will surprise the murderer and kill him.

Thus we see that the mitzvah of *eglah arufah* causes the murderer to be caught through [the publicity stirred by the ceremony]. My theory is supported by the fact that the land where the neck of the calf is broken may never be sown (*Devarim* 21:4). The owner of the site will do his utmost to search for the murderer, so the calf should not be killed and his land can remain productive.

> **RAMBAN** *(Devarim 21:5): According to this line of thinking, the ceremony holds only an indirect benefit [since it may lead to the capture of the killer], but the breaking of the calf's neck itself has no inherent purpose. If so, the ceremony should be in a fertile field, so that people will notice that it is not being tilled, rather than in a "harsh valley" where people do not notice that it is not tilled. In my view the reason for the eglah arufah ceremony is the same as that for sacrifices brought outside the Court of the Beis Hamikdash, namely, the goat sent to Azazel and the Red Cow. Therefore, the Rabbis counted the law of the eglah arufah among the* chukim *[laws whose reasons are not known].*

CHAPTER FORTY-ONE

PUNISHMENT

As we have mentioned, the benefit of mitzvos dealing with punishments meted out to offenders is well known, but now I will detail them specifically.

One who wrongs his neighbor is punished with the same thing being done to him. If he injures someone physically, he is made to suffer physically. If he damages someone's property, he is punished by the loss of property, although the owner of the damaged property can waive his claim for compensation totally or partially if he so desires.

Only a murderer is shown no clemency, and no ransom may be accepted from him, as it says, *When blood is shed in the land, it cannot be atoned for, except through the blood of the person who shed it* (*Bamidbar* 31:33). Even if the murder victim languished after the attack for some time, and in full control of his faculties, said, "Forgive my murderer; I have pardoned and forgiven him," we may not follow his instructions. We must take a life for a life, whether the victim was a child or an adult, a slave or a freeman, a wise man or a fool, because there is no greater crime than this.

One who mangles someone's limb, must himself lose a limb, as it says, *If one maims his neighbor, as he did so shall be done to him* (*Vayikra* 24:20). Of course our sages interpret this to mean that the perpetrator makes monetary compensation and does not actually lose his limbs, but my purpose is to explain the Torah verses, rather than the words of the sages. Non-the-less I can also explain to you these words of the sages, when we meet in person.

Payment is imposed for injuries that cannot be duplicated, as it says, *He must pay for the victim's loss of work, and must provide for his complete cure* (*Shemos* 21:19).

If someone damages another person's property, he must lose that much of his own property. [If an unpaid custodian misappropriated the item he was guarding,] *The person whom the court declares guilty must make double restitution to the other* (*Shemos* 22:6). [The custodian] must restore what he took, adding an equal amount to it from his own property.

Punishment as a Deterrent

The more prevalent a crime is and the easier it is to commit, the harsher must be its punishment in order to act as a deterrent; while crimes that occur infrequently need a less severe punishment. For this reason, a thief who stole a sheep must pay four sheep, which is twice as much as the fine for stealing other items,[20] though this only applies when he has slaughtered or sold the sheep (*Shemos* 21:37). Sheep are usually in the pasture and therefore cannot be watched as carefully as things kept in town. One who stole a sheep would sell it quickly before the theft could be discovered, or slaughter it so it could not be identified. Since stealing sheep was rampant, the punishment was severe.

The compensation for a stolen ox is [to pay five oxen,] which is greater by one-fourth, because stealing an ox is easier. Sheep stay together when they feed and they can be watched by the shepherd, so they can only be stolen at night. But oxen are scattered about when they graze, and a shepherd cannot watch them properly.

Similarly, what plotting witnesses wish to do to someone else is done to them. For plotting the death sentence on a person, they are put to death; for wishing to inflict lashes, they receive lashes; for trying to cause someone monetary loss, they are fined that amount. Thus, the punishment is equal to the crime, which is why the judgments [of the Torah] are called "righteous" (*Devarim* 4:8)

A robber is not required to pay a fine (*Vayikra* 5:23); only [if he denies the robbery under oath], does he pay an additional fifth, as

[20] For stealing other items the thief must pay double (*Shemos* 22:3).

an atonement for swearing falsely rather than as a fine for the robbery. This is because robbery happens infrequently since it is only possible in town with great difficulty. However theft is committed more often since it can be done everywhere. A thief can steal exposed or hidden things, while a robber can only take exposed things. One can protect himself from a robber, but he can't do so against a thief. Additionally, the robber is known and he can be arrested and forced to return the goods he robbed, whereas a thief is not known. For all these reasons the Torah fines the thief and not the robber.

Four Types of Sin

The severity of a punishment and whether the pain inflicted is harsh or mild depends on four conditions:

Firstly, the magnitude of the sin. Actions that cause great harm are punished severely, while actions that cause less harm are punished less severely.

Secondly, the frequency of the crime. A crime that is often committed must be stamped out with a harsh sentence; crimes that rarely occur can be restrained with a lenient punishment.

Thirdly, the degree of temptation. Only fear of severe punishment will restrain us from actions that are very tempting, whether we desire them greatly, we are accustomed to doing them, or they relieve great pain.

Fourthly, a deed that is easy to do furtively, which will go unnoticed, can only be deterred by the fear of a great and dreadful punishment.

Four Kinds of Punishment

The Torah divides punishments into four categories: (1) The death penalty pronounced by *beis din,* the court of law. (2)

The punishment of *kareis,* which is excision of the soul or premature death. (3) Flogging with a strap. (4) Prohibitions that do not involve action which are not even punished by flogging. Sometimes people are punished with flogging [even when their sin did not involve an action]. This includes a person who swears in vain, because he fails to recognize the exaltedness of G-d; one who substitutes an animal for one previously chosen as an offering to G-d, since this will lead him to disdain sacrifices dedicated to G-d; and one who curses a person by the name of G-d, because many people fear the effect of a curse more than they fear bodily harm. The transgression of other negative commandments that do not involve action cause little harm and cannot always be avoided, since the sin only entails words. Besides, if a person were flogged for each transgression of this kind, his back would be lashed continually. Moreover, it is impossible to give advance warning when dealing with a sin consisting of words.

Flogging

Although the Torah dictates that a sinner receives [forty] lashes (*Devarim* 35:3), this is the maximum number of lashes anyone can receive even if he is robust enough to withstand a hundred lashes, however, each man receives only as many lashes as he can bear, though not exceeding forty.

Kareis

There is no court-imposed death sentence for violating any of the dietary laws, for no great harm is done, and the temptation to eat non-kosher food is not as great as the temptation for illicit sexual relations.

However, the prohibition of eating blood is harshly condemned in the Torah, and the punishment is *kareis* [obliteration of the soul;

premature death]. (*Vayikra* 27:26). This is because in ancient days people were eager to eat blood since it was used in idolatrous ceremonies, as described in the book Tumtum.

The punishment of *kareis* is also given for eating *cheilev* [fats], because people enjoy eating *cheilev*, and because *cheilev* was offered on the altar [in the *Beis Hamikdash*].

Eating food on Yom Kippur and *chametz* on Pesach is also punishable with *kareis*. [Only a punishment as severe as *kareis* could deter people from violating these laws] because they are difficult to keep. Additionally, fundamental principles of the Torah, including the belief in the miraculous redemption from Egyptian bondage and the belief in repentance, are instilled by the laws of Pesach and Yom Kippur, as it says, *On this day you shall have all your sins atoned* (*Vayikra* 16:31).

Death Penalty

Death by the court is the penalty for transgressions of our fundamental beliefs or for serious transgressions, such as, idolatry, incest, murder. Actions that lead to these transgressions incur the same penalty. For example, one who desecrates the Shabbos incurs the death penalty because Shabbos affirms our belief that G-d created the world. A false prophet and a rebellious elder are executed because of the great harm they cause.

A son, bold enough to strike or curse his father or mother is put to death because of his enormous audacity, and because he destroys orderly family life which is the cornerstone of civilization. A wayward and rebellious son is put to death (*Devarim* 21:18-21) because he will eventually [rob and] kill someone [to satisfy his voracious appetite]. He who steals a human being is killed, because he is also prepared to kill his victim (*Shemos* 21:16). Similarly, he who breaks into a house is prepared to murder [the householder] (*Shemos* 32:1).

These three people, namely, the wayward and rebellious son, he who steals and sells a human being, and he who breaks into a house, are condemned to death because they will eventually become murderers.

The death penalty is only provided for extremely great sins. Only those cases of incest and adultery that can easily be done, are readily accessible, or are exceptionally tempting are punished by death. The punishment for all other cases is *kareis*.

Similarly, not all forms of idolatry are punished by the death penalty; only fundamental acts of worship, such as praying to an idol, prophesying in its name, passing a child through the fire [of *Molech]*, consulting spirits, and practicing sorcery.

The Rebellious Elder

Because society cannot function without punishments and judgments it is necessary to interrogate witnesses, to appoint judges in every town, and to have a king who is respected, feared and capable of using all kinds of deterrents to back the authority of his judges.

Although I have discussed the reasons for the laws included in The Book of Judges, I find it necessary to clarify the law concerning the rebellious elder.

G-d knew that the laws of the Torah might be expanded in some cases or curtailed in others to keep pace with the changing times, places, events, and circumstances. He therefore warned against [indiscriminately] adding to or subtracting from [the mitzvos], saying, *Do not add to it, and do not subtract from it* (*Devarim* 13:1), for this would bring about a breakdown in the system of Halachah, leading people to believe that the Torah was not given by G-d. But permission was given to the sages and Great Court of each generation to make protective fences around the laws of the Torah, introducing precautionary rules to safeguard against transgression of the law. These precautionary rules were to remain in force for all times, as the Mishnah says, "Make a fence for the Torah" (Avos 1:1).

By the same token, permission was given to abolish certain mitzvos or to permit certain things that had been forbidden, if circumstances and events require it. But these mitzvos are repealed only on a temporary basis; not for all time, as we explained in the introduction to our Commentary on the Mishnah in the section on Temporary Rulings. Through this process the Torah remains immutable forever, with temporary amendments to meet the requirements of times and events. Should every rabbi have the power to make such modifications, people would become confused by the differences of opinion that would arise. G-d, therefore, ruled that only the Great Sanhedrin has this power, and whoever disagrees [with the Sanhedrin's ruling] must be put to death. For if any and every rabbi were allowed to dispute the decision of the Sanhedrin, this law would be useless.

Four Kinds of Transgressions

Transgression of Torah laws may be divided into four classes: (1) Accidental transgressions, (2) inadvertent transgressions, (3) sins done deliberately, and (4) sins done maliciously.

He who sins accidentally is free from punishment and clear of all guilt, as it says, *You must not impose any penalty on the girl [who was raped], since she has not committed a sin worthy of death* (*Devarim* 22:26).

But a person who sins inadvertently is to be blamed, for had he been careful he would not have erred. Although he is not punished, he needs atonement for his sin, and therefore brings a sin offering.

The Torah differentiates between a private individual and a king, *Kohen Gadol*, or halachic authority regarding mistaken rulings and actions. From this we infer that a person who acts wrongly, or who renders a wrong halachic decision guided by his own reasoning—except in the case of the Great Sanhedrin or the *Kohen Gadol*—is treated as one who sins intentionally rather than one who sins in error. A rebellious leader is therefore put to death, although he acted and taught according to his view. However, the Great Sanhedrin must teach according to its opinion, and if the opinion is wrong, the sin is considered one due to error. The Torah says about such a case, *If the entire community of Yisrael commits an inadvertent [violation]* (*Vayikra* 4:13). Our Sages said about this principle: A careless misinterpretation is considered tantamount to willful transgression (Avos 4:13), meaning that he who has studied insufficiently, and teaches and acts based on his flawed knowledge is considered to have sinned intentionally. This is because one who eats the fat of the kidneys thinking it is the fat of the tail, has not erred as seriously as one who knowingly eats the fat of the kidneys thinking that it is not forbidden.

The latter brings a sin offering when he acted on his flawed knowledge, despite the fact that he is almost an intentional transgressor. However, one who renders a halachic decision based on flawed knowledge is considered an intentional sinner; only the Kohen Gadol and the Sanhedrin are regarded as unintentional sinners in this case.

One who sins intentionally receives the punishment prescribed in the Torah, whether death, monetary payment or flogging. When he is not liable for punishment by Torah law, he receives lashes as prescribed by the Sages. . . .

A malicious sinner sins intentionally, brazenly, and publicly, to contradict and negate the Torah, rather than because he was overcome by desire or suffers from bad character traits. He must be killed since he wishes to argue with the Torah. About him it says, *he has blasphemed G-d* (*Bamidbar* 15:30). Our Sages said this verse refers to idol worshippers; an idolater surely negates the Torah, because only one who believes the world has always existed would serve an idol.

In my opinion, anyone who transgresses even [a minor sin, such as] eating meat together with milk, wearing *shaatneiz*, or shaving the corners of his head, to disgrace the Torah because he does not believe it is true, is included in one who has *blasphemed* G-d. He is put to death for rebelling against G-d, as the residents of the wayward city (Devarim 13:13-19) are put to death. The death penalty is not a punishment for their sins; rather it is their just desserts because they rebelled. The property of the residents of the wayward city are burned, whereas the property of those given the death penalty for their sins is inherited by the heirs, proving that the residents of the wayward city are punished with death because they rebelled [against G-d].

It is also my opinion that a community that intentionally and blatantly sins must be put to death. This is why Bnei Yisrael gathered an army against the tribes of Reuven and Gad when they thought they had *turned today from G-d* (*Yehoshua* 22:16).

Obliterating Amalek

The section on Judges [in *Mishneh Torah*] contains the mitzvah to wipe out the seed of Amalek. Just as one person is punished for his sin, so must a whole tribe or nation be punished, so that other nations will be afraid to sin, thinking, "We will suffer the same fate as that tribe." Even if a terrorist who does not care if he is punished for his heinous acts arises, no member of his tribe will join him in his rampage.

Since Amalek was the first to attack Yisrael with the sword (*Shemos* 17:8-16), we are commanded to obliterate his name through the sword. Ammon and Moav only plotted to harm Yisrael out of stinginess, so we are only forbidden to marry or socialize with them. These punishments are neither excessive nor too lenient, as the Torah clearly says, *according to his crime* (*Devarim* 25:2).

The Army Camp

This section also contains the mitzvah *to designate a place outside the camp*, and, *to keep a spike with your weapons*[21] (*Devarim* 23:12,13).

---

21 They must designate a place to be used as an outhouse and have a spike to cover their excrement.

The Torah wishes to train Yisrael in cleanliness, distancing him from filth and squalor, so he should not behave like an animal. Furthermore, by fulfilling this mitzvah the soldiers will realize that the *Shechinah* dwells among them, as it says, *For Hashem your G-d walks in the middle of your camp* (ibid. v.14).

This leads to a related concept. The verse also says, *Let Him not see anything obscene among you, and turn away from you* (ibid.), warning against the promiscuity which is common among soldiers in an army camp who have been away from home for an extended time. G-d therefore commanded certain mitzvos to make us aware that the *Shechinah* is in our midst, so we will thereby avoid sinful acts. Those who had nocturnal emissions were required to stay outside the camp until the evening, *and when the sun sets, he can enter the camp* (ibid. 23:12). Thus every soldier realizes that the camp must be like a sanctuary of G-d, leading people to the service of G-d and bringing order into their troubled social structure. This is in contradistinction to a pagan camp where the soldiers are bent on havoc and sin, seeking to harm others and take their property. This is based on the plain meaning of the Torah text.

The Woman Captive

The Gemara explains the law about marrying a woman captive (*Devarim* 21:10-14) this way: "The Torah made an allowance for human passion."[22] Nevertheless, this law holds a moral lesson for virtuous people as well. A soldier must bring [a woman captive] to a private place, as it says, *You must bring her home* (ibid), even if he is overcome by desire. He is not permitted to sexually assault her on the battlefield.

Similarly, our Sages say he may not have sexual relations with her a second time until her grief has subsided and she has come to

22 For if G-d would not make her permissible, he would marry her against the law (Rashi).

terms with her situation. She may not be prevented from mourning, crying, neglecting her appearance, and looking disheveled, as it says, *Mourning for her father and mother a full month* (ibid.); for mourners find comfort in crying and grieving to the point of total exhaustion, just as happy people find joy in all kinds of cavorting.

The Torah shows mercy toward [the woman captive], giving her permission to continue mourning and weeping until she is worn out. [The soldier] cohabited with her while she was still a non-Jew, and for thirty days she is allowed to practice her religion, even continuing her idolatrous rituals. If she does not want to accept the laws of the Torah after the month is up, she may not be sold or treated as a slave. The Torah is mindful of the fact that [the soldier] had sexual relations with her, albeit somewhat improperly because she was a non-Jew. Nevertheless, it says, *Since you violated her, you may not sell her for cash or keep her as a servant* (ibid.).

Thus, I have explained the moral lesson and the reason for every mitzvah in this section.

Chapter Forty-two

Fairness in Business

The mitzvos in the seventh class, listed in the laws of Judgments and the laws of Acquisitions in *Mishneh Torah,* describe fair business dealings between two parties. Each party must have the other's interest in mind, and neither should try to increase his share of the profit [at the expense of the other] or walk away with all the earnings.

Overcharging is forbidden; only the standard rate of profit may be charged. Halachah has set the limits of profit for a transaction to be valid. Even hurting someone's feelings by mere words, is forbidden.

The Four Custodians

The law about the four kinds of custodians (*Shemos* 22:6-14) is obviously fair. An unpaid custodian is free from any responsibility, for he watches his neighbor's property as a favor, without pay, and without deriving any benefit for himself. If any damage occurs to the property, the owner must bear the loss.

A person who borrows an object takes it only for his own benefit, while the owner lends it to him as a favor. [The borrower] is therefore responsible for everything. He must pay for any loss to the property.

If a person is paid for guarding the property or pays for using it, both he and the owner benefit by it. The losses must therefore be shared between them. The custodian pays if the property is stolen or lost, for this happens only when the custodian is lax in guarding the property. But the owner bears any unavoidable loss, for example, if the animal falls and breaks a leg, or is carried off by armed bandits, or if it dies.

The Hired Laborer

The Torah shows extreme kindness toward the hired laborer because he is a poor man. His wages must be paid promptly, and he may not be cheated out of what he is owed. Additionally, laborers, and even animals, must be allowed to eat of the food on which they are working.

Inheritance

The laws of inheritance, included in property laws, admirably teach that a person should not withhold goodness from those who deserve it. Knowing that he is destined to die, one should not begrudge his heirs by squandering his assets, but leave it to the one who deserves it most, *the closest relative in his family who shall then be his heir* (*Bamidbar* 27:11). It is clearly stated that children are first in line, followed by the brother, then the father's brother.

The father should give preference to his eldest son, because his love for him came first. He must not be guided by his impulse, as it says, *He must not give the son of the beloved wife birthright preference over the first-born who is the son of the unloved wife* (*Devarim* 21:15). The Torah stresses caring for relatives, as the prophet says, *A man of kindness brings good upon himself, but a cruel person troubles his flesh* (*Mishlei* 11:17).

The Torah also says, *I am commanding you to open your hand generously to your poor and destitute brother in your land* (*Devarim* 15:11). Our Sages speak highly of a person who is kind to his relatives, commending one who marries his sister's daughter. The Torah teaches us to help a relative, feeling sympathy for him even if he wronged us or is morally corrupt.

Reciprocating Kindness

The Torah says, *Do not despise the Edomite, since he is your brother* (*Devarim* 23:8). So too, if someone once helped you and is now in trouble, you must pay him back for his good deed even if he treated you badly afterwards. The Torah says, *Do not despise the Egyptian, for you were a stranger in his land* (ibid.), and everyone knows how badly the Egyptians oppressed us. See how many noble character traits we derive from these mitzvos!

Chapter Forty-three

Shabbos and Yamim Tovim

The reasons for the eighth class of mitzvos, included in the book of festivals [in *Mishneh Torah*,] are stated in the Torah. Shabbos provides rest from strain and exertion; thus one seventh of every person's life, whether he is small or great, passes in delight and rest. Furthermore, Shabbos impresses on our mind the fundamental belief that G-d created the world [out of nothing].

Yom Kippur

Fasting on Yom Kippur brings one to thoughts of teshuvah. Because Moshe descended Mount Sinai with the second Tablets, announcing to the people that G-d had forgiven their grave sin on this day, it was appointed forever as a day devoted to teshuvah and fervent prayer. All physical pleasure and care of one's body are forbidden. No work may be done; everyone recites prayers of confession and repentance.

Pesach and Shavuos

By contrast, the Yamim Tovim are days of joy and festive gatherings that are necessary for the wellbeing of people. The Yamim Tovim also promote brotherhood and fellowship in the community.

Each of the Yamim Tovim has its own purpose. The reason for celebrating Pesach is well-known.[23] It is a seven day holiday be-

[23] *Remember this day [as the time] that you left Egypt, the place of slavery, when Hashem brought you out of here with a show of force* (*Shemos* 13:3), and many similar passages.

cause seven days is the average cycle between the daily cycle and the monthly cycle,[24] and the Torah follows the pattern of the natural world.

Shavuos commemorates the Giving of the Torah. In order to highlight its significance, we count the days that passed since the previous Yom Tov, just as a person who expects his best friend on a certain day counts the days and even the hours. Thus, we count the days of the Omer, beginning with our departure from Egypt until the day of the Giving of the Torah, since this was the purpose of our exodus from Egypt, as G-d said, *I brought you to Me* (*Shemos* 19:4). Because the Giving of the Torah took place on one day, we observe Shavuos for one day. Were we to eat matzah for only one day, it would not be exciting enough for us to internalize the message it conveys, for we often eat the same food two or three days. But by eating [matzah] for seven days, its central idea becomes crystal clear.

Rosh Hashanah

Rosh Hashanah, a day of teshuvah when we are shaken from our lethargy, is likewise observed for one day. We blow the shofar on this day as we have explained in Mishneh Torah.[25]

The day serves as a preparation for Yom Kippur, as may be seen from the additional prayers of supplication that are recited during the Ten Days of Repentance between Rosh Hashanah and Yom Kippur.

Sukkos

So the uplifting message of Sukkos can truly impact the people, this Yom Tov of gladness and joy is observed for seven days. Sukkos is observed in the fall, when we are rested and free from the

---

24 Each phase of the moon is approximately seven days.

25 There it states that the message of the shofar is: "Awake from your sleep, you that sleep, and you that slumber, awake from your deep sleep."

pressures of farming, as is explained in the Torah, *when you gather your produce from the field* (*Shemos* 23:16). . . .

Additionally, it is comfortable to sit in the sukkah at this time of the year, since it is not too hot, and heavy rain does not fall.

These two Yamim Tovim—Pesach and Sukkos—teach important beliefs and moral lessons. On Pesach we remember the miracles G-d performed in Egypt, and Sukkos reminds us about the miracles that happened in the wilderness, so we can transmit these lessons to future generations.

The Yamim Tovim convey an important moral lesson: We must remember our misfortunes even during times of fortune, learning to thank Hashem profusely and conduct ourselves humbly. Therefore we eat matzah and bitter herbs on Pesach to remember what happened to us, and we leave our homes on Sukkos, living in huts like wretched desert people, reminding ourselves that this was our situation long ago, as it says, *for I had Bnei Yisrael live in huts when I brought them out of Egypt* (*Vayikra* 23:43). Only through Hashem's kindness and because of His promises to our forefathers Avraham, Yitzchak, and Yaakov, who were perfect in their beliefs and character traits, do we now we live in fine homes in the best and most fertile land. Indeed, one of the basic themes of the Torah is that all the good we have received and will continue to receive is due to the merits of the Patriarchs because *they kept Hashem's way, doing charity and justice (Bereishis* 18:19).

On Shemini Atzeres we leave the sukkah, bringing our joy to a climax in the comfort of our spacious, solid homes.

The Four Species

The Sages suggest a reason for the Four Species [*lulav, esrog, hadassim,* and *aravos*] based on the well-known figurative Aggadic interpretation, although this does not explain the literal meaning of the text. . .

I believe the four species evoke joy reminding us that we were brought from the wilderness, *an area where there are no plants, figs, grapes, or pomegranates; there is not even any water to drink* (*Bamidbar* 20:5), to a country brimming with fruit-trees and rivers. To recognize this, we take the most beautiful fruit of the land [*esrog*], the most fragrant branches [*hadassim*], the most beautiful leaves [*lulav*], and the best of the herbs [*aravos*].

The four species were plentiful in Eretz Yisrael in those days, so they were readily available for everyone. They also are good-looking and the esrog and the hadassim have a good scent. The lulav and the aravos do not smell good, but neither do they have a bad smell. Additionally, these species stay moist and fresh for seven days, which cannot be said of peaches, pomegranates, asparagus, pears, and the like.

Chapter Forty-four

Reminders

The ninth class of mitzvos, which are listed in the section of Love, [in *Mishneh Torah,*] are self-understood. Clearly, these services remind us constantly to keep all G-d's mitzvos and affirm our belief in Him, as every devout person should. These include the laws of prayer, reciting the Shemah, Grace after meals, the Priestly blessings, *tefillin, mezuzah, tzitzis,* acquiring a *sefer Torah,* and reading in it at designated times. These mitzvos instill noble thoughts within us.

Chapter Forty-five

The Beis Hamikdash

We have already explained the purpose of the tenth class of mitzvos listed in the laws of the Beis Hamikdash [in *Mishneh Torah*] concerning the vessels of the Beis Hamikdash and the men who perform the service. Because idolaters always chose the highest places on tall mountains for their temples and idols, Avraham chose Mount Moriah, the highest mountain in that region, to proclaim the Oneness of G-d. He turned westward during his prayers because [he saw prophetically] that the Holy of Holies was on the west side [of the Beis Hamikdash]. This is what our Sages meant when they said, "The *Shechinah* is in the West." Indeed, the Gemara in *Yoma* explicitly states that Avraham turned to the west side where the Holy of Holies was to be built, when he prayed.

It was the pagan custom at that time to worship the sun as a god, and everyone turned to the east, [the place of the rising sun], when praying. Avraham, therefore, turned to the west on Mount Moriah – toward the Beis Hamikdash – with his back to the sun. And when the Jews abandoned G-d and returned to their early warped beliefs, what did they do? *They stood with their backs to the Sanctuary of Hashem, with their faces turned to the east, they were bowing eastward to the sun* (*Yechezkel* 8:16).

The location Avraham chose in his prophetic vision was known to Moshe Rabbeinu and many others, for Avraham commanded his children that a house of worship should be built on that place. The Targum says, "And Avraham worshipped and prayed there in that place, saying to G-d: 'Here future generations will worship Hashem'" (*Bereishis* 22:14).

Why Yerushalayim is not Mentioned in the Torah

Why isn't this place mentioned explicitly, but rather only hinted at in the verse *There will be a site that Hashem will choose as the place dedicated to His name* (*Devarim* 12:11)?

Firstly, had the nations of the world known that G-d selected this site over all places in the world, they would have occupied it or launched a ferocious war to seize it.

Secondly, this prevented those occupying the place [before Bnei Yisrael entered the land] from ravaging it.

Thirdly, and most importantly, each of the twelve tribes would desire this place, leading to conflict and rebellion, like the revolt sparked by the desire for the priesthood.[26] Therefore, the Beis Hamikdash could not be built before an elected king ordered its construction, nipping any conflict in the bud. I have explained this in the section on Judges [in *Mishneh Torah*].

Angels, Prophecy, Torah

In those days idolaters built temples, placing idols in them and dedicating a form of worship to a specific star or sign of the zodiac. Therefore, G-d commanded us to build a Sanctuary to Him, placing in it the Ark with two tablets of stone, engraved with the commandments, *I am Hashem your G-d*, and, *Do not have any other gods before Me . . .* (*Shemos* 20:2,3). Belief in prophecy precedes belief in the Torah, for if there is no prophet there is no Torah. But a prophet only receives a prophetic vision through an angel, as it says, *The angel of Hashem called* (*Bereishis* 22:15), and, *The angel of Hashem said to her* (ibid. 16:11), and countless other instances. Even Moshe Rabbeinu received his first prophecy through an angel,

---

[26] Korach's rebellion (*Bamidbar* 16,17).

as it says, *Hashem's angel appeared to him in a flame of fire* (*Shemos* 3:2). It is therefore obvious that belief in the existence of angels precedes belief in prophecy which precedes belief in the Torah.

Since the Sabeans did not know of the existence of G-d, they thought the zodiac with its stars were timeless and everlasting entities, and that idols and *asheiros* trees derived powers from the stars, inspiring the prophets and speaking to them in visions to explain what was useful and what was harmful. I explained this when discussing the prophets of Baal and *asheirah*.

Wise men realized that there is a true One and Only G-d, a Being that is neither a physical body nor a physical force. He brought other spiritual beings, the angels, into being, but these angels are not part of the zodiac and the stars. These angels, rather than idols or *asheiros*, were the beings that conveyed true prophetic messages to the prophets. This makes it clear that belief in the existence of angels is linked to belief in the existence of G-d, and these beliefs, in turn, leads to belief in the truth of prophecy and the Torah.

G-d commanded [Moshe] to place the form of two angel-like *keruvim* (cherubs) over the Ark, so belief in the existence of angels would be ingrained in the people's mind. This belief ranks second in importance to belief in the existence of G-d; and belief in G-d and the angels leads to belief in prophecy and the Torah, and to renouncing idolatry. Had there been only one *keruv*, the people might have been misled into thinking it was G-d's image which they were to worship in the way of the idolaters, or that the *keruv* itself was a deity, and that there were two deities—G-d and the *keruv*. By making two *keruvim* and explicitly declaring, *Hashem is our G-d, Hashem is the One and Only* (*Devarim* 6:4), Moshe established belief in the existence of a multitude of angels, precluding the error of considering [the two *keruvim*] as deities.

The Menorah

In front [of the Ark] was the *Menorah* separated [from the Holy of Holies] by a curtain. It was an impressive sight, burning continuously in order to glorify and honor the Sanctuary. The Torah emphasizes regarding the Sanctuary with esteem and reverence; anyone seeing it should be overcome with awe, humility, and submissiveness, as it says, *[Safeguard My Shabbos and] revere My Sanctuary* (*Vayikra* 19:30). It is linked to the observance of Shabbos to highlight its esteem.

The Altar

The reason for the incense altar and the burnt-offering altar and its utensils is obvious, but I don't know the reason for the Table with the bread on it; until today I have not been able to find a purpose for this mitzvah.

Our Sages (Middos 3:4) explain that the altar may not be made of cut stones, nor may any iron tool be lifted up on it, because iron was created to shorten man's life [through swords], and the altar was created to prolong man's life. It is not right for something that shortens life to be lifted against something which prolongs life.

This is a nice Aggadic explanation, but the basic reason is so we do not imitate the idolaters who built their altars with cut stones. Instead, we make an altar of earth, as it says, *Make an earthen altar for Me* (*Shemos* 20:21). If it is impossible to make it without stones, the stones must be used in their natural state, without being cut.

The Torah also forbids setting up a decorated stone (*Vayikra* 26:1), or planting a tree near the altar of Hashem (*Devarim* 16:21) because we may not worship G-d the way the pagans worship their idols. This thought is expressed in the following passage: *Do not try to find out about their gods, saying: "Now, how did these nations worship their gods? I would like to try [such practices]"* (*Devarim* 12:30). We may not worship G-d the way the pagans worship their idols, as the verse continues, *because in worshiping their gods these nations committed all sorts of perversion hated by Hashem.*

The Honor of the Kohanim

The worship of Pe'or, prevalent among the idolaters of that time, consisted of uncovering one's nakedness. Therefore the kohanim were commanded to wear *linen pants to cover their nakedness* (*Shemos* 28:42), and precluded from climbing up to the altar with steps, *so that your nakedness not be revealed on it* (ibid. 20:23).[27]

As a sign of respect and honor, the Sanctuary was constantly surrounded [by Levi'im], who guarded it to prevent the ignorant and unclean from entering. No one could enter while drunk, unclean, or with uncut hair and disheveled garments; furthermore, every kohen washed his hands and feet before officiating.

The kohanim and the Levi'im who performed the service in the Beis Hamikdash were greatly honored, enhancing its eminence. To distinguish the kohanim, they wore *holy garments that are dignified and beautiful* (*Shemos* 28:2). A kohen with a blemish was not allowed to officiate, and kohanim afflicted with a deformity were disqualified from performing as kohen, since the masses judge a person by his looks and clothing rather than his true form [i.e., his intellect and character,] as set forth in the laws of this commandment. The Beis Hamikdash and those serving in it must be revered by everyone.

The Levi'im did not offer sacrifices, nor could they convey atonement. Only kohanim were agents for atonement, as it says, *The kohen shall make atonement* (*Vayikra* 4:26), and, *The kohen shall then make atonement for her* (ibid. 12:8). The Levi'im sang [in the Beis Hamikdash], and therefore a Levi became unfit to serve when he lost his voice. The Levi'im's choir stirred the people's feelings for the service in progress. Emotions were roused by the harmonious melodies [chanted by the Levi'im] accompanied by the orchestra which always played in the Beis Hamikdash.

As a sign of reverence, even the kohanim who were fit [to serve] were precluded from sitting down while on duty in the Beis

[27] Instead, they ascended the altar with a ramp (*Rashi*).

Hamikdash, or entering the Sanctuary whenever they wanted. No one ever entered the Holy of Holies except the Kohen Gadol, and he entered it only four times on the day of Yom Kippur. These rules increased the grandeur of the Beis Hamikdash.

The Incense

Since a great number of animal sacrifices were offered in the Beis Hamikdash every day, with the flesh cut into pieces and the intestines washed and then burned, no doubt it could smell like a slaughterhouse if things were left to take their course. In order to give the place and the garments of those who served there a pleasant scent, the Torah commanded [the kohanim] to burn incense twice every day, once in the morning and once in the evening.

The Sages said: "The fragrance of the incense [burnt in the Beis Hamikdash] could be smelled as far away as Yericho." This also increased respect for the Beis Hamikdash, since good odors raise our spirits, while bad smells repel and nauseate us.

Reverence for the Beis Hamikdash

The anointing oil served a dual purpose—permeating the anointed object, whether a man, garment, or vessel, with a good odor, and extending an exalted, holy, and exceptional aura to it. This also evoked respect for the Beis Hamikdash which in turn led to fear of G-d. Entering the Beis Hamikdash, a person's cold heart melted, and he became submissive as G-d planned. With a softened and humble heart, the people would accept G-d's mitzvos and fear Him, as it says, *You must eat this before Hashem your G-d in the place that He will choose as dedicated to His name. There you shall eat [the second] tithe of your grain, wine, and oil, as well as the first-born of your cattle and smaller animals. You will then remain in awe of Hashem for all time* (*Devarim* 14:23). The purpose of all these observances is now clear.

We are not allowed to reproduce the anointing oil and the incense because its fragrance should be smelled only in the Beis Hamikdash, making a uniquely powerful impact. Additionally, [if anyone could prepare the anointing oil], a person might anoint himself with it thinking this made him a holy man. This would lead to fights and contention.

Acts of Respect

The Ark was carried on the shoulder and not placed on a wagon, as a sign of respect. It was forbidden to change the Ark's appearance, so even the carrying poles were not allowed to be removed. Likewise, the *eifod* and the breastplate were not allowed to be separated.

The priestly garments were entirely woven, rather than being cut [and then sewn] in order not to spoil the work of the weaving.

Those who officiated in the Beis Hamikdash were forbidden to perform each other's tasks, since not doing the specific duty assigned to them could lead to overall negligence and sloppiness.

Different areas of the Beis Hamikdash, such as, the *Har Habayis,* the *Chil* [outer circuit], the Women's Court, the Courtyard, and so on, up to the Holy of Holies, had different degrees of holiness, thus increasing the respect that everyone who approached the Beis Hamikdash had for it.

We have explained the reason of all the mitzvos in this class.

Chapter Forty-six

Sacrifices

I have already reviewed [in chapter 32] the mitzvos of the eleventh class, discussed in the Book of Service and the Book of Sacrifices [in *Mishneh Torah*] in general terms. Now I will give a reason for each mitzvah, as I understand it.

According to the Onkelos translation, the Torah says the Egyptians worshiped Aries [the Ram, the first sign of the zodiac,] and therefore prohibited the killing of sheep and despised shepherds. And so Moshe said to Pharaoh, "*Could we sacrifice the sacred animal of the Egyptians before their very eyes, and not have them stone us?*" (*Shemos* 8:22), and Yosef said, *Since all shepherds are despised by the Egyptians* (*Bereishis* 46:34).

A popular form of worship amongst some Sabean sects was the worship of demons in the form of goats, called *se'irim* (goats). Thus it says, *They will then stop sacrificing to the* se'irim *who continue to tempt them* (*Vayikra* 17:7). For this reason, these idolatrous sects prohibited eating goat's meat. And out of great esteem for cattle, most idolaters opposed the killing of these animals. Indeed even today, you will find that the people of India do not slaughter cattle, even in regions where other animals are slaughtered. To neutralize these false beliefs we were specifically commanded to offer these three animals, as it says, *The sacrifice must be taken from the cattle, sheep or goats* (*Vayikra* 1:2). What idolaters considered the worst crime, we use as a means to become close to G-d, obtaining forgiveness for our sins. Thus their evil ideology, the disease of the human soul, is transformed into a cure.

Animal, Bird, and Flour Offerings

To cleanse us from these spurious beliefs, and publicize the message [of belief in G-d], we were commanded to kill a lamb on Pesach, sprinkling its blood on the entry doors, proclaiming [to the Egyptians] that the very act they consider the cause of death would be the cause of our rescue from death, as it says, *Hashem will pass over that door and not let the angel of death enter your houses to strike you* (*Shemos* 12:23). The Jews were rewarded for boldly performing the act that the idolaters considered a heinous crime.

This is why these three animals [cattle, sheep and goats] were chosen to be brought as offerings. Furthermore, these three species of domestic animals are readily available, whereas the idolaters sacrificed lions, bears, and wild beasts of the desert, as is mentioned in the book Tumtum.

Since many people cannot afford to offer an animal, the Torah allowed birds to be sacrificed as well. [The Torah chose] turtledoves and pigeons, birds that are abundant in Eretz Yisrael, and easily obtained. One who could not afford a bird could bring any sort of bread prepared in the style of those days, either baked in an oven, or fried in a pan or deep bowl. If baking bread was too difficult for him, he could bring flour, or even choose not to bring an offering, for the Torah says explicitly that refraining from bringing an offering is not considered a sin, *If you refrain from making vows, then you will not sin* (*Devarim* 23:13).

Offerings in the Beis Hamikdash

The idolaters offered leavened bread, sweetening their sacrifices with honey, and omitting salt from their offerings. The Torah therefore prohibited us from offering leavened bread or honey, and commanded us to salt every offering saying, *You must offer salt with all your sacrifices* (*Vayikra* 2:13). The Torah also commanded us to offer perfect sacrifices, to keep from showing disdain or contempt for something offered to G-d, as it says, *When you present a lame or sick animal, is nothing wrong? Present it, if you please, to your governor. Would he be pleased with you and show you favor?* (*Malachi* 1:8).

For this reason one could not offer an animal that had not yet lived seven days (Vayikra 22:26), for it is flawed, considered like an aborted fetus. Similarly, it is forbidden to offer a prostitute's compensation and the exchange of a dog because both are despicable. Frankincense was used because its scent is pleasing in places filled with the odor of burnt flesh. The burnt offering was skinned and its intestines and legs washed, although they were entirely burned afterwards, because this showed proper respect for the offering, so it should not appear disgusting. This concept is stressed repeatedly, as it says, *You defile [the offerings] saying: "The table of Hashem is loathsome," and by your description of it as, "its food is repulsive"* (*Malachi* 1:12).

This is also why an uncircumcised or unclean person was not allowed to partake of any offering, and why an offering that had become unclean could not be eaten.

Offerings had to be consumed in a specific place within an allotted time frame, or they could not be eaten. Nothing was eaten from the burnt-offering since it was entirely devoted to G-d. Sin-offerings and guilt-offerings were only eaten in the Court of the Beis Hamikdash, on the day and the night following the slaughtering. Peace-offerings which were of lesser sanctity could be eaten anywhere in Yerushalayim on the day they were offered and on the following day, but after that time, the offerings would spoil and become unfit to eat.

The Kohen's Minchah Offering

The meal offering of a kohen was completely burned (*Vayikra* 6:16), because the kohen himself offered it; were he to eat it after offering it, it would seem as if he had not performed any service at all. The *minchah* offering of a private person consisted only of frankincense and a handful of flour or cake; if the person who brought this puny size offering also ate it, the service would be unnoticeable.

Korban Pesach

The *korban pesach* must be roasted over fire and eaten in one house without breaking any of its bones (*Shemos* 12:9), because the primary principle for these laws was, *You must eat it in haste* (*Shemos* 12:11). Just as the matzah symbolized the hurried departure of the Jews, so was roasting the fastest way to prepare the pesach lamb; there was no time cook it into a prepared dish. So too, breaking the bones to extract the marrow was forbidden because when you are rushed, there is no time for that. Likewise, carrying food from one house to another is also time consuming, so the *korban pesach* must be eaten in one house. The purpose of these mitzvos was to rush so no one should be late and miss the departure of the entire people thereby risking attack from the plots [of the Egyptians]. These mitzvos were made permanent so we can remember what happened, as it says, *This law must therefore be kept at its designated time from year to year* (ibid. 13:10).

One needed to reserve a share of the *korban pesach* before it was slaughtered. This forced people to buy it ahead of time, rather than relying on a relative or friend to invite him.

According to the Sages, an uncircumcised male is forbidden to eat from the *korban pesach* because the Jews neglected the mitzvah of *milah* while they were in Egypt in order to assimilate with the Egyptians. When they were given the mitzvah of the *korban pesach* Bnei Yisrael were commanded that no one could sacrifice the *korban* unless he, his son, and the male members of his household had undergone *milah*, as it says, *Then he may join in the observance* (ibid.12:48). The blood from the great number of men who underwent *milah* because of this commandment, mingled with the blood of the *korban pesach*. The verse, *Then I passed you and saw you wallowing in your blood, and I said to you, "In your blood shall you live; in your blood you shall live"* (*Yechezkel* 16:6), refers to the blood of the *korban pesach* and the blood of *milah.*

Idolatrous Blood Rituals

Although the Sabeans regarded blood as unclean, they ate it because they believed it was the food of demons; by eating it they would connect to demons who would reveal future events to them. Because some people were unable to eat blood, since it is repulsive to human nature, they gathered the blood of any animal they killed in a bowl, eating the flesh of the animal while sitting around the [the bowl filled with] blood. They imagined the demons eating the blood, which is their food, while they [the idolaters] ate the flesh, because sharing a meal with demons would create companionship, whereby the demons would appear to them in their dreams, notifying them about coming events, and generally being helpful to them. People were fascinated by these ideas; no one doubted their validity.

The perfect Torah, to eliminate this pernicious spiritual disease, likened the prohibition of eating blood to idolatry, stating, *I will direct My anger at the person who eats blood and cut him off spiritually from his people* (*Vayikra* 17:10). The same language is also used in reference to one who gives of his seed to Molech, *Then I will direct My anger at him* (ibid. 20:5). These words are only used for idolatry and the eating of blood, since eating blood leads to the worship of demons which is a kind of idolatry.

[In contrast] the Torah declared that blood is pure, and made sprinkling blood the means of purifying objects, as it says, *Sprinkle it on Aharon and on his vestments, and on his sons . . . This will consecrate Aharon as well as his vestments and his sons* (*Shemos* 29:21). Furthermore, blood was sprinkled on the altar, and the service consisted of pouring out the blood rather than collecting it, as it says, *He shall spill out all [the rest of] the blood at the base of the sacrificial altar* (*Vayikra* 4:18), and, *The blood of your sacrifices shall be poured on the altar of Hashem your G-d* (*Devarim* 12:27). The blood of every non-sacrificial animal that was slaughtered was also poured out, as it says, *You must spill it on the ground like water* (*Devarim* 12:16). The Torah forbids gathering around blood and eating there, as it says, *Do not eat around the blood* (*Vayikra* 19:26).

RAMBAN *(Vayikra 17:11,12): Though the Rambam's remarks are reasonable, the text does not bear this out. Rather the verses say that the reason [eating blood is prohibited] is,* For the life of any creature—its blood represents its life *(17:14), and,* For the soul of the flesh is in the blood, *and,* Only be strong not to eat the blood—for the blood, it is life, and you shall not eat the life with the meat (Devarim *12:23).*

This is the proper explanation for the prohibition against eating blood: Hashem created all living things in this world for the benefit of man, because man is the only one who recognizes his Creator. Yet, in the beginning G-d allowed Adam to eat only vegetation, but no living creatures, as it says, G–d said, "Behold, I have given you every seed-bearing plant . . . (Bereishis *1:29).*

After the Flood, when the animals were saved in the merit of Noach, he brought [animals] as a korban *to G-d which He accepted. At that time G-d permitted man to slaughter [animals for food], as it says,* Every moving things that lives shall be to you as food; like plant vegetation I have [now] given you everything (Bereishis *9:3), because the animals survived [the Flood] in the merit of man. Because animals owe their life to man, G-d permitted man to eat and derive benefit from their bodies. He also ordained that the soul [i.e., the blood] of animals should be used for man's atonement when he offers them as* korbanos *for Hashem. But man is not allowed to eat [blood], because a creature that has a soul should not eat another creature's soul, since all souls belong to G-d. Both the life of man and the life of an animal belong to G-d,* because they have one and the same fate, as the one dies so does the other, and both have the same life-breath (Koheles *3:19). The Greek philosophers believe that a dazzling radiance burst forth at Creation, emanating the spark that is the soul of the animal. Therefore animals have a real soul which endows them with the instinct to run away from harm, seek out things beneficial for them, and recognize and love familiar people, just as dogs love their masters and easily recognize the members of their master's family. Pigeons, too, have some intelligence and recognize familiar people.*

It is known that food is absorbed in the body, so that the food and the one who consumes it become one flesh. Consequently, if one eats the blood of an animal, the animal's blood is absorbed by one's own blood, blending with it. Blood does not need digestion like other foods which are first broken [into soluble substances absorbable by tissues], thus one's soul fuses with the animal's soul. As a result, the soul becomes insensitive and crude, akin to the animal's soul [which is present in the blood] he ate, as it says, Who knows that man's spirit does rise upward and a beast's breath sinks down into the earth? (Koheles *3:21). Therefore it says,* For the soul of all flesh is in the blood *(17:11), which means: The soul of all flesh—whether man or beast—is in the blood, and one cannot mix the soul that is destined for destruction [i.e., the animal's soul] with the soul that lives on [after death]. Instead, [the soul of the animal] should serve as atonement on the altar to be acceptable before Hashem.*

This is the intent of the verse, Therefore I have said to Bnei Yisrael, "Let none of you eat blood" (Vayikra *17:12): Since blood is the same as the soul it is not right for one soul to consume another soul. But G-d having compassion on man's soul, gave [the animal's soul] to him to be placed on the altar, to atone for man's soul.*

Prohibition of non-Sacrificial Meat

Because the people continued in their rebelliousness, tending toward the popular beliefs in which they had been raised, and assembling around the blood in order to eat it and thereby associate with demons, G-d prohibited them from eating ordinary meat throughout their stay in the wilderness, permitting only the meat of peace-offerings. This was commanded so the blood should be poured out on the altar, and the people should not gather around it, as it says, *Bnei Yisrael shall thus take the sacrifices that they are offering in the fields and bring them to Hashem, to the Communion Tent entrance. They can then be offered as peace offering to Hashem . . . And the kohen shall sprinkle the blood on the altar. Bnei Yisrael will then stop sacrificing to the demons [who continue] to tempt them* (*Vayikra* 17:5-7).

Because non-domestic animals were never sacrificed, and birds were never used as peace offerings, the Torah commanded that whenever a permitted non-domestic animal or a bird was killed, its blood must be covered with earth, so people would not gather around the blood to eat there. Thus the bonds between these demented lunatics and their demons were broken.

This [idolatrous] doctrine flourished around the time of Moshe Rabbeinu, captivating and deceiving the people, as stated in *parashas Haazinu: They sacrificed to demons who were non-gods, deities they never knew. These were new things, recently arrived, which their fathers would never consider* (*Devarim* 32:17). The Sages explained the words *non-gods* as follows: "Not only have they failed to stop worshiping things that exist, they even worship imaginary things." Sifri puts it as follows: "It is not enough for them to worship the sun, the moon, and the stars; they even worship their shadows."

The prohibition of slaughtering non-sacrificial animals applied only in the wilderness, because it was commonly believed that demons materialized in the desert, but did not appear in cities and populated areas. City folks who wanted to perform any of those insane rites had to leave town for barren and desolate places. Therefore, the use of non-sacrificial meat was permitted after they [left the desert and] entered Eretz Yisrael. Furthermore [by the time they reached Eretz Yisrael] the disease [of idolatry] had tapered off, and this doctrine had fewer followers. Moreover, it was almost impossible for everyone who wanted to eat meat to come to Yerushalayim. For these reasons, "non-sacrificial meat" was forbidden only [during Yisrael's stay] in the wilderness.

The Offering Fits the Sin

The greater the sin a person committed, the lower the class of animal used for his sin offering. There is no sin greater than idol worship, and no species inferior to a female goat, because the female of the species is always inferior to the male. Thus, only a female goat could be offered for the sin of inadvertently worshipping idols, but an ordinary person could bring either a ewe-lamb or a female goat (*Vayikra* 4:27-35) for other sins. Out of respect for his high rank, a king's offering for inadvertent sins was a male goat (ibid. 22-26). Because the transgressions of a *kohen gadol* or the Sanhedrin involved legal decisions, rather than actions, they brought a bull as an offering for inadvertent sins; when their [faulty] decision dealt with idolatry (*Bamidbar* 15:24) they brought a male goat.

Meal-Offering of a Sinner and a Sotah

Sins which required guilt offerings were not as grave as sins which required sin offerings, therefore guilt offerings were a male ram or a male lamb, with both the species and the sex [of the guilt offering] on a superior level. For the same reason, burnt offerings, which were entirely consumed on the altar, were only male animals.

Following this principle, oil and incense were not added to the meal offering of a sinner or a *sotah* (a woman suspected of adultery), since they were brought by people who behaved improperly. Their offering reminds them to repent, implying, "Your offering is lacking any enhancement because of your evil deeds." Since the *sotah* behaved more disgracefully than one who sinned unwittingly, her offering consisted of barley flour, the lowest of species. And herewith, the reasons for all these laws are provided in a wonderful fashion.

Sin Offering

Our Sages say the sin offering of the calf brought on the eighth day of the dedication [of the *Mishkan*], atoned for the sin of the golden calf, as did the sin offering of the bull brought on Yom Kippur.

From the words of our Sages, I infer that goats were brought as sin offerings, by individual persons and by the whole congregation on the Yamim Tovim, Rosh Chodesh, and Yom Kippur, because Bnei Yisrael's rebelliousness usually consisted of sacrificing to demons [who were called *se'irim* – goats.] The Torah mentions this in so many words, saying, *They will then stop sacrificing to the* se'irim *who continue to tempt them* (*Vayikra* 17:7).

Equivalence

Our Sages explain that the goats used as sin offerings for the congregation alluded to their sin of selling the righteous Yosef, as it says, *They slaughtered a kid of a goat* (*Bereishis* 37:31). Be mindful of this, and realize that the purpose of all offerings was for the sinner to recognize his sin, as [David] said, *My sin is constantly before me* (*Tehillim* 51:3), understanding that he and all his future offspring must seek atonement for the sin through an offering similar to the sin he committed.

Thus, if a person sinned with his property, he must generously spend his property in the service of G-d. If he indulged in sinful bodily enjoyment, he must wear down his body, afflicting it with fasting and [decreased sleep] by rising before daybreak. If he sinned through bad moral and ethical conduct, he must practice the extreme opposite behavior, as we explained in *Mishneh Torah, Hilchos Dei'os.*

If he sinned by thinking wrongful thoughts and believing erroneous doctrines because of his failure to study, he must remedy his fault by turning away from worldly affairs, focusing exclusively on abstract thoughts and thoroughly studying the correct principles of our belief, as it says, *My heart was seduced in secret, but my hand pressed against my lips* (*Iyov* 31:27). These words metaphorically instruct us to pull back from issues that seem doubtful, as we explained in the beginning of this treatise.

Thus, since Aharon erred with the sin of the golden calf, the Torah ordained that he and his successors bring a bullock and calf as an offering. So too, when [the brothers] sinned with a goat-kid [when they sold Yosef], their atonement was through a goat-kid.

People who understand this concept, will recognize that disobeying the will of G-d is a grave sin. They will distance themselves from sin to avoid the lengthy and exhausting process of atonement; aware that even that process cannot guarantee forgiveness, they will do their best to avoid sin. The benefit of this line of thinking is obvious.

The Offering of Rosh Chodesh

The goat offered as a sin offering on Rosh Chodesh is called *chatos laShem*, "a sin offering to Hashem" (*Bamidbar* 28:15). However, the goats of the sin offerings on the three Yamim Tovim and any other sin offerings are not so described. The *mussaf* offerings, brought by the community at special times, were all burnt offerings and therefore called, *isheh laShem*, "a fire offering made to Hashem" (*Bamidbar* 28:19 et al). Only one goat as a sin offering, eaten by the kohanim, was offered on these special days. The Torah does not speak of "a sin offering to Hashem" and "a peace offering to Hashem" because these offerings were eaten by man. Even sin offerings that were entirely burned cannot be called "a sin offering to Hashem," as we will explain. It was therefore impossible for the goats brought on the Yamim Tovim, which were eaten [by the kohanim] and not entirely burned, to be called "a sin offering to Hashem."

Avoiding a Misunderstanding

But the goat offered on Rosh Chodesh, might be mistaken to be a sacrifice to the moon, since the Egyptians sacrificed to the moon on the day of its monthly reappearance. Idol worshippers sacrificed to the new moon, just as they sacrificed to the sun when it rose to a certain inclination above the horizon, as described in their books. Therefore the Torah states explicitly that the goat of Rosh Chodesh is offered because Hashem commanded it, and it is not a sacrifice to the moon. Therefore, the phrase *a sin offering to Hashem* is used in connection with the goat brought on Rosh Chodesh, to repudiate the idolatrous notions that had gained a foothold in the ailing hearts of the Jewish people. We do not fear this misconception will arise when the sin offerings of the Yamim Tovim were sacrificed, because those sin offerings were not given on the days of the new moon, or indeed on any day associated with a natural phenomenon. Rather, they were offered on days designated by the Torah. Take note of this remarkable insight.

The Burning of the Sin-Offering

Sin-offerings brought to atone for great sins, such as the sin-offering of the king who inadvertently violated certain negative commandments, are burned outside the camp, rather than on the altar (*Vayikra* 4:21). Only burnt-offerings and the like may be offered on the altar, which is why the altar is called "*altar of the burnt-offering*" (*Shemos* 30:28), for their smell is an *appeasing fragrance to Hashem* (*Vayikra* 2:9), since they remove idolatrous beliefs from our hearts, as we have explained.

Sin-offerings are burned, hinting that the sin for which the offering was brought has been completely eliminated, just as the burned body [of the offered animal] has disappeared. No trace remains of the sinful deed, just as no trace remains of the burned sin-offering. A sin offering did not produce *an appeasing fragrance to Hashem;* on the contrary, its smoke is despicable. Therefore the burning of the sin offering took place outside the camp. Similarly, the Torah describes the meal offering of the *sotah* as, *a reminder offering to recall sin* (*Bamidbar* 5:15). Which is not a pleasing thing [to G-d].

The Goat to Azazel

Since the goat sent [into the wilderness on Yom Kippur] (*Vayikra* 16:20), served as atonement for all serious transgressions, more sins than any other communal sin-offering, it was considered as though it bore all sins and therefore, was not accepted as an ordinary sacrifice to be slaughtered, burnt, or even brought near the Beis Hamikdash. It was removed as far as possible to a desolate, barren, and uninhabited area. Of course, sins are not a burden to be transferred from a person's back to the back of the goat. Rather, these ceremonies are symbolic actions to inspire the people to do teshuvah, as if to say: We have cleansed ourselves from all past sins, casting them behind our backs and removing them from us as far as possible.

Meat, Wine, and Music

I am puzzled, unable to understand, why G-d commanded wine to be offered. Since the idolaters offered wine, [one would expect it to be forbidden to be brought on the altar, like leaven and honey]. But although I am unable to explain it, someone else suggested the following reason: The desire for food is situated in the liver, and meat is its greatest source of satisfaction. Man's vitality is situated in the heart, and wine is the most powerful stimulant for the heart. The soul which is rooted in the brain derives its greatest pleasure from music. Therefore, each of these faculties offers to G–d what it desires most, namely, meat, wine, and song.

Yamim Tovim

The purpose of observing the Yamim Tovim [and going to Yerushalayim to celebrate them] is well-known. These gatherings inspire people with a renewed love for Torah, besides strengthening the bonds of friendship and companionship. This is especially true of the mitzvah of *Hakheil*, when [every seven years,] the entire nation gathered together on Sukkos, as it says, *They will thus learn to be in awe of Hashem, carefully keeping all the words of this Torah* (*Devarim* 31:12).

An Abundance of Food in Yerushalayim

For this same reason, money for the second tithe must be spent in Yerushalayim, and the fruit of trees in their fourth year and the tithes of the cattle had to be brought to Yerushalayim. Since the meat of the tithes, the wine of the fruit of the fourth year, and the money of the second tithe, would be in Yerushalayim, there would always be an abundance of food there. None of these things could be sold, nor could any be set aside for another year, for the Torah orders that they be brought *each year* (*Devarim* 14:22), forcing the owner to give part of it as *tzedakah*. The Torah stresses the importance of giving tzedakah on the Yamim Tovim, saying, *You shall rejoice on your festival, along with your son and daughter, your male and female slaves, the Levi'im, proselytes, orphans, and widows from your settlements* (ibid. 16:14).

We have explained the reason for every mitzvah and many of their details in this class.

Chapter Forty-seven

Ritual Purity

Although we have briefly mentioned [in chapter 35] the mitzvos of the twelfth category, which are in *Sefer Taharah* of *Mishneh Torah,* we will offer additional explanations to show the reason for each mitzvah.

The sole purpose of G-d's Torah, revealed to Moshe Rabbeinu and called [*Toras Moshe*] by his name, is to make the service [of G–d] less burdensome. Only because he is unaware of the [idolatrous] customs and beliefs that were rampant in those days, does a person complain that certain mitzvos cause him hardship or strain. Consider the difference: A heathen had to burn his own son to serve his god, as the Torah states, *In worshiping their gods, these nations . . . would burn their sons and daughters in fire* (*Devarim* 12:31). And instead of such a sacrifice our service of G-d entails the burning of a pigeon or a handful of flour!

With this thought in mind, G-d rebuked Yisrael when they were disobedient, saying, *My people, what [wrong] did I do to you, and how did I tire you? Testify against Me!* (*Michah* 6:3), and, *Have I been a wilderness to Yisrael, or a land of deep darkness? Why have My people said, "We separate ourselves from You; we will no longer come to You"* (*Yirmeyah* 2:31). The prophet meant to ask: What mitzvos of the Torah have become burdensome to Yisrael that they turned away from it? In the same spirit G-d cries out, *What wrong did your forefathers find in Me, that they distanced themselves from Me* (ibid. 2:5)? All these verses have one underlying theme, which answers many questions]. Keep it in mind!

Revere the Beis Hamikdash

The main idea behind [the design] of the Beis Hamikdash was to inspire the people with awe and reverence, as it says, *Revere My sanctuary* (*Vayikra* 19:30). Since seeing an object over and over again, no matter how exalted it may be, decreases your respect for it, making the excitement it once evoked wear thin, the Sages discouraged frequent visits to the Beis Hamikdash, citing the verse, *Let your feet be scarce in your fellow's house* (*Mishlei* 25:17).

Therefore the Torah forbids [ritually] unclean people to enter the Beis Hamikdash. Considering the many sources of impurity, few people were actually clean. Even if a person did not touch the carcass of a dead animal, he [probably] touched one of the eight creeping animals whose dead bodies are frequently found in homes, in food and drink, and may be stepped on wherever we walk. And even if he avoided touching these, he may have touched a woman during her days of ritual impurity, or a man afflicted with a leprous disease, or perhaps their beds. If he avoided these, he may have become unclean by having marital relations with his wife, or by seminal discharge. Even after cleansing himself of these impurities, he could not enter the Beis Hamikdash until after sunset. One is not permitted to enter the Beis Hamikdash at night, so he may have had relations with his wife again, or come in contact with some form of ritual impurity during the night and awaken the next day in the same situation he was the previous day. All this caused people to stay away from the Beis Hamikdash, preventing them from entering it at their pleasure. Our Sages made this well-known comment: "Even a clean person may not enter the Beis Hamikdash in order to perform a service, unless he first immerses in a *mikveh*." This contributed to an aura of respect [for the Beis Hamikdash], evoking an exhilaration that brought the desired humility . . .

These laws have many benefits. Firstly, they keep us away from filthy and disgusting things. Secondly, they guard the Beis Hamikdash. Thirdly, they show consideration for a healthy lifestyle, in contradistinction to the Sabeans who imposed bothersome restrictions on cleanliness, as you will soon hear. Fourthly, [the Torah laws] lightened our burden, for they do not restrict our daily occupation, since the laws of purity and impurity apply only to the Beis Hamikdash and to the holy things connected with it, as it says, *She shall not touch anything holy, and shall not enter the sanctuary* (*Vayikra* 12:4). A person [who does not go to the Beis Hamikdash] is not guilty of any sin. He may remain unclean as long as he wishes, eating non-holy food that has become unclean to his heart's content.

Burdensome Sabean Practices

The Sabean customs persist even today among the Magus—the few surviving worshipers of fire in the countries of the East. [According to their custom,] a menstruating woman must stay alone in the house, the places she stepped on have to be burned, whoever speaks with her becomes unclean, and even if a wind passes over her and a clean person, that person becomes unclean. Note the great difference between their practice and our precept: "During her menses a wife may do any work she usually performs for her husband. Only marital intercourse is forbidden during the time of her impurity."

Another Sabean custom that has survived to the present time is considering anything separated from the body, such as hair, nails, or blood, to be impure. According to their line of thinking every barber is unclean because he touches blood[28] and hair, and whoever shaves with a razor has to immerse in running water. The Sabeans had many such onerous practices, whereas we apply the laws of purity and impurity only to holy things and to the Beis Hamikdash.

[28] Barbers did bloodletting.

According to Sifra, the Torah verses, *Since I am holy, you must remain holy* (*Vayikra* 11:44), and, *You must be holy* (ibid. 19:2), do not refer to the laws of purity, but rather to obedience to G-d's mitzvos. Transgressing the mitzvos is called "unclean," and "impure" with the word "impure" used especially for transgressing the three cardinal sins of idolatry, adultery, and murder. In regard to idolatry it says, *He has given his children to Molech, thus defiling that which is holy to Me* (ibid. 20:3). Concerning adultery it says, *Do not let yourselves be defiled by any of these acts* (ibid. 18:24), and, in reference to murder it says. *You must not defile the land upon which you live* (*Bamidbar* 35:34) . . .

TZARAAS—LEPROSY

We have already explained, and the Sages have also expounded that *tzaraas* is a punishment for slander. The disease begins in the walls of one's home. If the [slanderer] does teshuvah, the purpose is achieved, however if he continues to slander, the *tzaraas* affects his bed and his furniture. If he persists in his evil way, the disease spreads to his garments, and finally, attacks his body. This was a known miracle, similar to the water of the *sotah* [the suspected adulteress] (*Bamidbar* 5:11), whose significance was known to the people. The benefit of this miracle is obvious. Besides, *tzaraas* is a contagious disease, and people have an inborn loathing to it.

The *metzora* was purified through a process involving a piece of cedar wood, hyssop, crimson wool, and two birds (*Bamidbar* 14:4). The reason explained in the Midrash does not coincide with my viewpoint. I do not know the reason for these things, nor why cedar wood, hyssop, and crimson wool were used in the offering of the red cow, nor why a bunch of hyssop was required to sprinkle the blood of the *korban pesach* [on the beam and the two doorposts] (*Shemos* 12:22). . . .

Chapter Forty-eight

Forbidden Food

The mitzvos included in the thirteenth category are mentioned in the laws of Forbidden foods, the laws of Slaughtering, and the laws of Vows and nazirite vows. In Tractate Avos we explained the benefits of this group. Now we will elaborate on the specifics of the individual mitzvos.

In my opinion, all foods forbidden by the Torah are harmful to one's health.[29] No one doubts that eating any food the Torah forbids is unhealthy; however, there are some who doubt that pig's meat and hard fat are harmful. But they are wrong, for pig's meat contains an excess of moisture and an excess of indigestible nutrients and waste material. Pig's meat is forbidden because this animal wallows in filth and eats loathsome things, and Scripture expresses revulsion about squalor even in the countryside, and surely in town. If pig's meat were permitted, our streets and houses would be dirtier than an outhouse, as may be seen in the homes of today's Frenchmen. Our Sages put it as follows: The mouth of a pig is as dirty as excrement.

The fat of the intestines makes us feel bloated, harms the digestion, and causes cold and pasty blood. It should be used as fuel rather than food. Blood and *neveilah* (an animal that died a natural death) are harmful and indigestible, and a *tereifah* (an organically defective animal) will eventually become a *neveilah*.

Chewing the cud and split hoofs for cattle, and fins and scales for fish are merely the identifying signs for permitted animals. In

---

[29] The Rambam, one of the greatest Torah scholars of all time, was also an outstanding physician who was appointed court physician to Sultan Saladin of Egypt. In his medical writings he describes many conditions, including asthma, diabetes, hepatitis, and pneumonia.

and of themselves, they are neither the cause for permission when they are present, nor of prohibition when they are absent. They are signs to distinguish acceptable from unacceptable species.

The reason the *gid hanasheh* (displaced nerve) is forbidden is written explicitly in the Torah (*Bereishis* 32:35).

It is forbidden to cut off and eat a limb of a living animal (*Devarim* 12:23) because this fosters brutality and cruelty. Additionally, pagan kings did this, and it was also done in idolatrous ceremonies.

Meat and Milk

Undoubtedly, meat boiled in milk is a heavy food that makes a person overfed. I think it may also be prohibited because it was connected with idolatry, perhaps forming part of the service or used in a ritual at some pagan festival.

My hypothesis is supported by the Torah twice mentioning this prohibition following the commandment concerning the Yamim Tovim, *Three times each year every male among you must appear before Hashem . . . Do not cook meat in milk* (*Shemos* 23:17, and *ibid* 34:23,26), as if to say: "When you come before Me on your festivals do not cook your food the way the idolaters used to cook it." Though I think this is the most convincing reason for the prohibition, I have found no mention of this pagan ritual in any of their writings.

Kindness to Animals

Vegetables and meat are man's natural food, and the best meat is from those animals we are permitted to eat, as every doctor knows. Because an animal must be slaughtered to obtain this good food, the Torah commands that we kill the animal in the most humane method. Therefore we are forbidden from slicing the throat in a harsh manner, piercing it, or cutting off a limb while the animal is alive.

It is forbidden to slaughter a female animal and its offspring on the same day (*Vayikra* 22:28), to ensure that the mother does not see her young being slaughtered, since that would cause her pain. There is no difference between the pain of a person or an animal in such a case, because maternal love stems from the imagination which man has in common with most animals, rather than the intellect. This law applies only to cattle and sheep, the only domestic animals allowed to us, since it is these animals that recognize their young.

> **RAMBAN** *(Devarim 22:6): According to the Rambam, the prohibition against killing a mother and its young should apply only if one killed the young before its mother. However, the Torah also prohibits killing the mother before the young. According to this line of reasoning we must say that killing the mother before the young was prohibited as a preventive measure so one won't come to kill the young before the mother. I think a more correct reason for this prohibition is to keep us from being heartless.*

Likewise, we chase away the mother bird before taking her young, for a mother bird who is sent away won't feel pain when the young are taken. Incubating eggs and chicks in need of their mother are usually not fit for consumption, so this law often causes a person to drop the entire project. If the Torah decreed that we spare cattle and birds from grief, surely we must not cause pain to our fellow man.

> **RAMBAN** *(Devarim 22:6): The reason for the commandment of sending away the mother bird before taking the young, and prohibiting the slaughter of a cow and its calf on the same day is not because G-d had pity on them. His mercies on animals do not reach the point of preventing us from using them for our needs.*

> *Were that the case, G-d would forbid us to slaughter them. The reason for the prohibition [against taking the mother bird together with its young and slaughtering the cow and its calf on the same day] is to instill in us the trait of compassion, teaching us not to be cruel, because such acts tend to make a man cruel. Evidence of this is the fact that butchers who slaughter large oxen and donkeys are extremely vicious by nature. For this reason the Sages (Kiddushin 82a) said, "The worthiest of butchers is Amalek's partner."*

The sages said that if one prays, "Just as G-d had mercy on the bird so should he have mercy on us," he is silenced, because he is labeling the commandments as merciful laws when in fact they are decrees. This implies that the reason for this mitzvah is not mercy, contradicting our explanation. This dictum is based on the opinion that there are no reasons for the mitzvos and they were only given so we can fulfill G-d's will. However, we are of the second opinion who believes there are reasons for the mitzvos.

We have already explained [in chapter 46] why we cover the blood of a slaughtered bird or wild animal, and why this rule applies only to fowl and wild animals.

Vows

In addition to the foods prohibited by the Torah, we are commanded to observe the prohibitions we impose on ourselves by making vows. If you say, "This bread or piece of meat is forbidden for me," you are not allowed to eat that food. This law trains a person in moderation, curbing his desire for food and drink, as the Sages explain, "Vows are a fence for abstinence." If women were in control of their own oaths, their sensitive and excitable natures could cause tension, quarrel, and turmoil in the family. [If she made an oath to abstain from a certain food], one kind of food might be allowed for the husband, yet forbidden for the wife; another kind might be forbidden for the daughter yet permitted for the mother. Therefore, the father of the family controls things that affect the welfare of the household. A mature, independent woman, who is of age and has no husband or father, is subject to the same laws as a man.

It is well-known, that the laws of the *nazir* make a person abstain from wine, which has caused untold calamity throughout the ages. [As it says,] *Many strong men have been slain by it* (*Mishlei* 27:26), and, *For they, too, have erred because of wine and strayed because of liquor* (*Yeshayah* 28:7). As an additional safeguard, these laws prohibit eating anything derived from the grape, its seeds or its skin. A nazir is even prohibited from drinking wine of necessity [such as *kiddush* wine]. Because the holiness of a person who abstains from wine equals that of a *kohen gadol*, the *nazir*, like the *kohen Gadol*, may not defile himself for his [deceased] father or mother. He acquires this lofty stature because he abstains from wine.

Chapter Forty-nine

Marriage

The fourteenth category of mitzvos, which are found in the Book of Women, are the laws of forbidden sexual relations, the laws of mingling species, and Milah.

Man needs friends all his life, as Aristotle states, "When one is content and in good health, he enjoys the company of friends; in time of adversity he needs them, and in his weak, old age, they help him." The love that exists between parents and children and among relatives is a deeper love than the affection [of friends]. Genuine brotherly love and the readiness to lend a helping hand can be found only among close family members. People who share a grandfather and even descendants of a common distant ancestor love one another, help each other, and have pity on each other. Promoting familial love is a main purpose for the Torah's [marriage] laws.

Prostitution

Therefore the Torah forbids prostitution (Devarim 23:18), which destroys the record of one's lineage. A prostitute's child is a stranger to everyone. The child does not know any relatives, and no one acknowledges kinship with him. This is the worst thing that can happen to a father and his child.

Additionally, prostitution increases lust, because new affairs and experiences with different types of people excite one more than experiences to which one is accustomed, therefore it was also prohibited to prevent excessive desire for sexual intercourse.

The ban on prostitution prevents quarreling. Several men visiting the same woman can easily be incited to violence, often to the point of killing one another or the woman. This has happened ever since antiquity, as it says, *They converged on a harlot's house (Yirmeyah 5:7)*. In order to prevent these terrible evils and ensure that everyone knows his lineage, prostitution was outlawed.

Betrothal and Wedding

Sexual relations are permitted only after a man chooses a woman and marries her publicly. If merely choosing a woman were enough, a man could bring a prostitute to his home for an agreed upon period of time, saying she is his wife. Therefore, the Torah commands that a man perform a ceremonial act of *eirusin* (betrothal) declaring the woman to be his future wife. Then he publicizes the betrothal by marrying her in the *nisu'in* (marriage) ceremony,[30] as it says, *And Boaz took ten men* (*Ruth* 4:2).

Sometimes, a marriage fails, and the couple's mutual love and peace evaporates. If that happens, the husband is permitted to divorce his wife. However, were he allowed to divorce her by merely uttering a few words, or by turning her out of his house, [without the need for a written document to substantiate the divorce], the wife would look for [the husband to commit] some oversight, [so she could leave him] and claim to be divorced. Or, if she committed adultery, she and the adulterer might claim she had been divorced. Therefore, the Torah decreed that divorce is only possible by means of a document certifying the breach, as it says, *He shall write her a bill of divorce* (*Devarim* 24:1).

The Suspected Adulteress

It frequently happens that a husband suspects his wife of adultery or has misgivings about her fidelity. Because the Torah has laws

30 In our present-day wedding ceremony, *eirusin/kiddushin* and *nisu'in/chuppah* are combined.

concerning [the *sotah,*] the woman suspected of adultery (*Bamidbar* ch.5), every married woman, out of fear of the "bitter waters," will be extremely careful not to arouse her husband's resentment. Even an innocent and pure woman would rather part with all her possessions than undergo the ordeal [of the *sotah*], preferring death to the terrible shame of having her head uncovered, her hair undone, and her garments torn until her heart is exposed, while she is paraded through the entire Sanctuary in full view of the Sanhedrin and other women and men. The fear of this [trial] prevents the ruination of many a blissful home.

Seduction

Since every young girl expects to marry, one who seduces a girl is required to marry her, for he is the most suitable husband for her, healing her wound and restoring her reputation better than any other husband. However, if she or her father reject him, he must pay the dowry (*Shemos* 22:16). As an additional punishment, a man who molests a girl, *may not send her away as long as he lives* (*Devarim* 22:29).

Yibbum and Chalitzah

Yibbum, marrying your deceased brother's wife, was an ancient custom which the Torah preserved *So that his [brother's] name may not be obliterated from Yisrael* (*Devarim* 25:6).

The ceremony of *chalitzah*—taking off the shoe[31]—was considered shameful. Therefore [it encouraged *yibbum* because] a person might decide to marry his deceased brother's widow to avoid this disgrace. This can be seen from the words in the Torah, *This is*

---

[31] If the brother does not wish to go through with the marriage, the widow removes his shoe freeing her to marry. See *Devarim* 25:1-9.

what shall be done to the man who will not build up a family for his brother. The name [of this place] shall be known in Yisrael as, "the house where the shoe was removed" (*Devarim* 25:10).

YEHUDAH'S INTEGRITY

Yehudah's behavior [toward Tamar] teaches us decency and fairness. *"Let her keep the security," said Yehudah. "We don't want to be put to shame. I tried to send her the kid, but you could not find her"* (*Bereishis* 38:23).

Sexual intercourse with a prostitute before the Torah was given was as lawful as marital relations between husband and wife after the Torah was given, being perfectly permitted. The payment for a harlot's services in those days corresponds to the *kesubah* of our days, payable to a wife upon her divorce. The wife is entitled to it, and the husband is required to pay it.

Yehudah said, *Let her keep the security; we don't want to be put to shame,* showing that conversation about sexual relations—even when permitted—is shameful and we should keep quiet about them, even if the silence results in monetary loss. Thus, Yehudah was saying: I'd rather suffer a loss and let her keep what she has, than publicize our affair by trying to find her, thereby bringing shame on us. We can learn this lesson in decency from Yehudah's conduct.

Yehudah's conduct also holds a lesson in honesty. He did not rob her, nor did he go back on his word and break the agreement he had made with her. For he said, *I tried to send her this kid, but you could not find her* (*Bereishis* 38:23). The kid was surely a good one, therefore he pointed to it, saying, *this kid.* He displayed the integrity he inherited from Avraham, Yitzchak, and Yaakov, [who taught] that one may not go back on one's word or break an agreement; and one must always give to others all that it due to them. It makes no difference whether the money is a loan, wages, or being held for safekeeping.

KESUBAH

A husband must give his wife a *kesubah* (marriage contract) equivalent to the wages one pays a hired worker. There is no difference between a master who withholds the wages of a hired man and a husband who deprives his wife what is due her. Moreover, there is no difference between a master who wrongs a hired servant and then brings charges against him intending to fire him without pay, and a husband who fabricates charges against his wife so he can divorce her without paying the *kesubah.*

THE DEFAMED WIFE

The Torah laws pertaining to a husband who invents charges against his wife are fair. Surely the man perpetrating this evil did not love his wife. Had he chosen to divorce her properly, nothing would have stood in his way. However, in order to rid himself of her without paying her the *kesubah* due to her, he invented charges against her. He defamed her, falsely accusing her of things she did not commit, to save himself the fifty shekels of silver the Torah obligates for a *kesubah.* Therefore he must pay her one hundred shekels of silver, in accordance with the principle, *The person whom the courts declare guilty must then make double restitution to the other* (*Shemos* 22:8), similar to the law about plotting witnesses, as we have explained above. Since [the husband] plotted to cheat her of fifty shekels of silver, he must add fifty and pay her one hundred shekel as punishment. Furthermore, as punishment for disgracing her by rumoring that she was guilty of adultery, he is disgraced by receiving lashes, as it says, *and [the city elders] shall chastise him* (*Devarim* 22:18). Finally, as punishment for lustfully seeking pleasure, he must keep her as his wife forever, *and he may not send her away as long as he lives* (ibid. 22:19), since this happened because she was ugly in his eyes. Thus are his bad habits cured through the laws of G-d.

Wisdom and Fairness of G-d's Laws

The laws of the Torah are fair and righteous. One who slanders his wife, to deprive her of his obligatory payments, is treated like a thief who stole his neighbor's property. A plotting witness who schemed to inflict damage is punished like a thief and slanderer who have actually caused damage, although the plotter did not actually inflict damage. *One Torah and one judgment* (*Devarim* 32:4) is sentenced to all three sinners. The Torah says, *The deeds of the Mighty One are perfect, for all His ways are just* (ibid. 32:4). Stand in awe of the wisdom contained in G-d's laws and admire His wonderful deeds! Just as His works are absolutely perfect, so are His laws absolutely just, although our mind is too limited to grasp the perfection of all His works or the fairness of all His laws. However, just as we are able to understand some of His wonderful works, for example, in the organs of animals and the movement of the zodiac, so can we understand the fairness of some of His laws. Of course, the little we know is greatly superseded by what is unknown to us.

Forbidden Relations

The laws about forbidden sexual relations teach us to limit sexual intercourse, desiring it only on rare occasions. If the natural act is base, to be performed only out of necessity, how much more so if it is performed in an unnatural manner, only for the sake of pleasure. Thus the prohibition against homosexual relations and intercourse with beasts (*Vayikra* 18:22) is self-explanatory.

A man may not marry his female relatives since they are constantly with him in the house, and can easily be swayed to do what he desires. They are close at hand and readily available to him, with no judge able to prevent him from being in their company. Were he allowed to marry any of them, precluded from having sexual intercourse with them only without marriage, as is the case with other unmarried women, most men would constantly be guilty of engaging in illicit sexual relations with them. Therefore these women were completely forbidden, with sexual intercourse severely punished by death and *kareis* (excision of the soul). Because such intercourse is never lawful, we have reason to believe that men will not lust after [their female relatives].

Included in this prohibition, are one's wife's mother or sister, and a step-daughter or step-granddaughter born from one's wife. These women are with her most of the time, easily accessible, and the husband will see them as he exits and enters [his home] and even while working. Similarly a wife is often together with her husband's brother, father, or son, because we generally enjoy the company of our sisters, aunts, and the wives of our uncles, often being raised together with them. Therefore we are forbidden to marry these close relatives. . . .

RAMBAN *(Vayikra 18:6): To make a man liable to kareis merely because these women are in the house with him, while allowing him to marry as many as hundreds and thousands of women, seems like a weak reason. . . .*

We don't have a tradition to explain the reason for forbidden relationships. It seems to be a mystical secret relating to the transmigration of souls. The Torah frowns on sexual intercourse permitting it only for the preservation of the human race. Intercourse which cannot result in a child is forbidden. Intercourse which would produce an abnormal offspring is also forbidden. This is implied by the words any kin of his own flesh, *and,* for his own kin he has laid naked *(Vayikra 20:18). The Torah forbids these unions because the close kinship would result in unhealthy offspring. Therefore their relationship is lewdness and cannot be a marriage.*

Accordingly, forbidden sexual relationships are chukim, "decrees of the King," stemming from the King's knowledge. He runs His Kingdom with wisdom, knowing the necessity and benefits of the commandments He gives.

The reasons it is forbidden to have sexual relations with a menstruating woman (*Vayikra* 18:19) and with another man's wife (ibid. 20) are obvious and need no further explanation.

Erotic Thoughts

We are forbidden to take any pleasure from a woman who is prohibited to us; even looking at her if we intend to derive pleasure from her is prohibited, as we explained in "Laws about Forbidden sexual relations" (*Mishneh Torah* ch.21:1-2). The Torah forbids us from thinking about sexual intercourse or arousing the male organ. Should a man unintentionally become sexually aroused he must turn his mind to other thoughts until his sexual excitement subsides. Our Sages exhorted: "My son, If this abominable villain [the *yetzer hara*] grabs you, drag him to the *beis hamidrash*. If he is made of iron, he will melt, and if he is made of stone, he will crumble into pieces, for it says, *Behold, My word is like fire—says Hashem—and like a hammer that shatters a rock* (*Yirmeyah* 24:29)." The Sage [of the Talmud was] telling his son, "If you suffer from sexual excitement, go to the *beis hamidrash* and study; by taking part in the discussions and asking and answering questions, the suffering will surely wane." The term "abominable villain" is aptly used, for what an abomination this [*yetzer hara*] is!

The philosophers teach the same lesson as the Torah, scorning people who lust after sexual intercourse and desire food delicacies, denouncing their objectionable way of life. Aristotle said, "The sense of touch which is our disgrace, leads us to indulge in eating and sexual intercourse." You will find this in his book on Ethics and in his book on Rhetoric.

Crossbreeding of Animals

Similarly, the Sages caution us not to look at animals or birds when they are mating, and this may be the reason crossbreeding of livestock is forbidden (*Vayikra* 19:19). Animals will not mate out of species, unless they are forced to do so, for example, by mule breeders. The Torah did not want a Jew to degrade himself with such coarse and shameless acts. If the Torah only hints to these actions, rather than mentioning them explicitly, certainly we should not engage in these actions. And, for that matter, crossbreeding is not necessary.

Harnessing two species of animals may be forbidden to avoid the mating of two species. Thus it says, *Do not plow with an ox and a donkey together* (*Devarim* 22:10), because they might mate if they are put together. Indeed, this commandment applies to other animals besides the ox and donkey; it is forbidden to plow with any two kinds of animals, although the Torah speaks only of the common occurrence [of an ox and donkey].

Circumcision

The mitzvah of *milah* weakens the male organ, reducing sexual relations.

Some people think *milah* corrects an inborn physical defect. But this theory can easily be refuted, for how can a natural organ be defective, needing to be repaired by human hands? Besides, the foreskin is useful for that organ.

The purpose of *milah* is not to remedy an inborn physical defect; it is a means of rectifying man's moral flaws. The wound of *milah* does not interfere with any of man's physical functions, nor does it impede his ability to father children. Rather, *milah* quells excessive sexual desire, mitigating its pleasure. The organ is bound to become weak when it loses blood and its covering is removed soon after birth.

Our Sages explicate: It is hard for a woman who had sexual intercourse with an uncircumcised man to separate from him. I believe this is an important reason for *milah*.

Who was the first to perform this mitzvah? Our father Avraham, who was known for his fear of sin. Our Sages mention this in connection with the verse, *[Abraham said to Sarah,] "I realize now that you are a good-looking woman"* (*Bereishis* 12:11).[32]

There is another important reason for the mitzvah of *milah*. All the men of our faith, who believe in the Oneness of G-d, sport a physical sign that unites them, making it impossible for a non-Jew to claim he is one of us. Were it not for this, a man might claim Judaism to gain some advantage or to mislead Jews. But no man would circumcise himself or his son unless he is motivated by true faith, for *milah* is not like a scratch on the leg or a blister on the arm; it involves difficult surgery.

People united by a sign symbolizing a mutual covenant will love and help each other. *Milah* is the symbol of the covenant that Avraham our father made for belief in the oneness of G-d. Everyone who is circumcised enters the covenant of Avraham to believe in the oneness of G-d, [as G-d said,] *to be a G-d to you and to your offspring after you* (*Bereishis* 17:7). This reason for *milah* is as important as, and perhaps even more important than, the first reason.

Milah on the Eighth Day

There are three reasons to perform this mitzvah when the child is very young. Firstly, a grown person may not want to undergo *milah*. Secondly, a baby does not feel much pain, since his skin is tender; and because his imagination is not developed he does not feel threatened, whereas an adult is terrified of things he imagines to be threatening. Thirdly, parents are not yet attached to a very young child because they cannot imagine him as a lovable, grown person. Their affection increases as he develops, though it wanes [as he reaches maturity]. Thus the parents' love for their new-born baby is not as great as it is when he is one year old, and when he is one year old, he is less loved by them than when he is six years old. If a child was not circumcised for two or three years, the father, whose duty

[32] Until now Avraham was not aware that she was beautiful, because of their extreme modesty.

it is to perform the *milah,* would not be able to perform the mitzvah, overwhelmed by his love and pity for the child. On the other hand, shortly after birth, the father's love for his infant is still weak.

Milah is performed on the eighth day because all living beings are weak and tender at birth, as if they were still in the womb; they are not considered viable, breathing humans until the end of seven days. This is also true for animals, as it says, [When a bull, sheep, or goat is born] *it must remain with its mother for seven days* (*Vayikra* 22:27), as if it were lifeless during that time. Therefore, a child is circumcised after seven days have passed, with no exception.

One of the Torah's *righteous rules and laws* (*Devarim* 4:8) is the prohibition of injuring the male sexual organs. We must always follow the middle course. Thus, although *milah* teaches us not to over-indulge in marital relations, neither should one abstain entirely, for the Torah commands, *Be fruitful and multiply* (*Bereishis* 1:22). Thus, the male organ is weakened by *milah,* but it is not disabled. The natural impulse is left intact, although shielded against overindulgence.

Forbidden Unions

A man with crushed testicles or a cut member (*Devarim* 23:2) may not marry a Jewish woman because their sexual relations would be pointless and futile. Obviously, such a marriage would be a stumbling block for both of them.

In order to curb the spread of unlawful unions, the Torah prohibits a *mamzer*[33] from marrying a Jewish woman, warning men and women that by committing adultery they inflict irreparable harm on their child. Children born of adulterous unions are disdained in every nation, but the Jewish people take pride in the fact that *mamzeirim* are forbidden to intermingle among them altogether.

[33] A *mamzer* is someone born of an adulterous or incestuous union. Someone born out of wedlock is not a *mamzer*.

Since *kohanim* have a higher sanctity, they may not marry a prostitute, a divorced woman, or a woman born of an illicit marriage with a *kohen* (*Vayikra* 21:7). The *kohen gadol*, the highest-ranking *kohen*, is also forbidden from marrying a widow or a woman who is not a virgin. Just as *mamzeirim* are forbidden to marry into the congregation of Hashem, so too, slaves and handmaids are prohibited.

The reason for the prohibition of marrying a non-Jew is explicit in the Torah – if you marry them, you or your children will ultimately serve idols.

Prevention of Idol Worship

The purpose for most *chukim*—statutes whose reasons are hidden—is to prevent idol worship. Because we understand things we actually witness more than things we only hear about, it is difficult for me to explain some details and the purpose [of the idolatrous practices], since my knowledge of the Sabean cult, which has been gone for more than two thousand years, is derived from books; it is not as reliable as the knowledge of an actual witness to those [idolatrous] practices. If we knew all the details of the Sabean worship and belief, we would understand the reason and recognize the wisdom in every detail of the Torah laws regarding sacrifices, ritual uncleanness, and other laws whose reasons seem obscure. These laws cleared a man's mind of false beliefs, eradicating idolatry which wasted people's time, turning their minds from intellectual research and constructive action. The prophet Shemuel described the idolatrous lifestyle as, *pursuing futilities that cannot avail and cannot rescue, for they are futile* (1 *Shemuel* 12:21), and Yirmeyah said, *It was all falsehood that our ancestors inherited, futility that has no purpose* (*Yirmeyah* 16:19). Consider how much harm [idolatry] causes; should we not do our utmost to put an end to this evil?

The Correct Mental Outlook

I have already established that the mitzvos serve to erase [corrupt] beliefs, easing the heavy burden, pain and affliction brought on by idolatry. If you do not know the reason for any positive or negative mitzvah in the Torah, you may surmise that it is a remedy for the disease [of idol worship] which we do not suffer from today, thank G-d. This is the correct outlook of a person who knows the true meaning of the Divine pronouncement, *I did not tell the descendants of Yaakov to seek Me for nothing* (*Yeshayah* 45:19).

Summary

I have explained the mitzvos in these [fourteen] classes, delineating reasons for all of them, with the exception of a few mitzvos and some minor details. However, a thoughtful reader can infer the implied reason of even these [unexplained mitzvos].

Chapter Fifty

The Importance of Historical Data

Some sections in the Torah contain profound mysteries which have been widely misinterpreted, especially chapters in the Torah that seem pointless, such as the chronicles of the families descended from Noach with their names and their lands; the descendants of Seir, the Chori; the kings that ruled in Edom, and the like. The Gemara (*Sanhedrin* 99b) relates that the wicked king Menasheh held wild parties at which he ridiculed these passages, blasphemously saying, "Did Moshe have nothing better to write in the Torah than [such useless trivia as] *Lotan's sister was Timna* (*Bereishis* 35:22)?"

I will give you a general rule [about all such passages], and then explore them one by one, as I have done in giving reasons for the mitzvos.

Every story in the Torah is important, either teaching a fundamental principle of belief or containing an ethical or moral lesson to prevent wrongdoing and injustice.

A fundamental principle of the Torah is that the world was created out of nothing, and that *Adam Harishon* was the first human being. The time span between Adam and Moshe Rabbeinu was about 2500 years. If [the story of creation in Bereishis] was the only information available, people may have doubted its veracity, because the human race is spread over all parts of the world and it consists of various nations speaking different languages. Therefore, the Torah describes the genealogy of the nations, explaining that originally they all dwelled in one place and spoke the same language, as would be expected of descendants of one person, but eventually the families branched away from one another. The Torah explains why they were dispersed to the four corners of the world and why they spoke so many different languages, mentioning who the famous men among them were, who their fathers were, and how long and where they lived.

The stories of the flood and the destruction of Sedom and Amorah teach us that *There is, indeed, fruit for the righteous; there is, indeed, a G-d who judges in the land* (*Tehillim* 58:12).

Through a miracle, Avraham and a few untrained men defeated four mighty legions in the war of the nine kings (*Bereishis* ch.14). Then Avraham risked his life to rescue his nephew Lot who shared his beliefs. This story teaches that Avraham was satisfied with his lot, spurning wealth and working hard to attain the highest moral qualities.This is illustrated with his words, "*Not thread nor a shoelace! I will not take anything that is yours*" (*Bereishis* 14:23).

Eisav, Se'ir, Amalek

The Torah relates the chronicles of the families of Se'ir (*Bereishis* 36:1-30) and their lineage because G-d commanded Yisrael to wipe out the nation of Amalek, the son of Elifaz and Timna, the sister of Lotan (*Bereishis* 36:12). Yisrael was not commanded to destroy the other descendants of Eisav. The Torah explicates that Eisav was related by marriage to the families of Se'ir ((*Bereishis* 36:25), had children with them and reigned over them. His offspring intermingled with theirs, and eventually all the countries and families of Se'ir were called after the sons of Eisav who were the predominant family. They adopted the name of Amalek, because the Amalekites were the bravest in that family.

Had the lineage of the families of Seir not been listed in full, we would have assumed all of them were Amalekites, and mistakenly killed them all. Therefore, the Torah identifies their families, implying that the people living today in Se'ir and in the kingdom of Amalek are not all Amalekites; they are otherwise descended, but are called Amalekites because [Timna] the mother of Amalek was of their tribe. This is an example of G-d's righteousness; the decree [to annihilate Amalek] was meant only for the offspring of Amalek, so He prevented the killing of [innocent] people who lived among other people [marked for extermination].

A reporter's account of an event differs from a witness's account. An observer will see many important details that can only be told with detailed descriptions. Though the reader may find the account repetitive, a witness to the event would see the need for every detail. Therefore, we tend to think stories in the Torah with no connection to any mitzvah are unnecessary, rambling, or redundant, but had we witnessed the incident we would understand its importance.

Journeys in the Wilderness

The summary of Bnei Yisrael's journeys [in the wilderness] (*Bamidbar* chapter 33), seems unnecessary at first glance. Therefore, the Torah says, *Moshe recorded their stops along the way at Hashem's command* (*Bamidbar* 33:2). It was essential that they be recorded, so future generations recognize the validity of the miracles that happened. Only witnesses to a miracle believe they are true beyond doubt; later generation may consider them legends or myths, denying they actually occurred. Miracles do not endure for generations, yet Bnei Yisrael stayed in the wilderness, *where there were snakes, vipers, scorpions, and thirst, because there was no water* (*Devarim* 8:15) forty years, finding manna there every day. This is one of the greatest miracles recorded in the Torah. They lived far from civilization, in places not fit for normal life, *an area where there are no plants, figs, grapes or pomegranates* (*Bamidbar* 20:5), *a land through which no one passed and where no person settled* (*Yirmeyah* 2:6). There, as the Torah says, *You neither ate bread nor drank wine* (*Devarim* 29:5). These are obvious miracles that everyone can see.

But G-d knew people would harbor doubts about these miracles in time to come, just as people cast doubts on the truth of other stories. Perhaps they would decide Bnei Yisrael stayed in the wilderness close to an inhabited area where they could live a normal life, such as the desert regions where Arabs live today, or that they plowed and harvested the land in the places they lived, or subsisted on some vegetation that grew there. [Or people may think that] manna always came down naturally, or that there were wells of fresh water in those places. In order to quell any doubts and validate the miracles, the Torah lists all the journeys, enabling future generations to learn about the great miracle when human beings survived in the wilderness for forty years.

For the same reason Yehoshua cursed anyone who would ever rebuild Yericho (*Yehoshua* 6:25), so [the memory of] the miracle [of the wall falling down] should endure forever; whoever saw the wall sunk in the ground would realize it was not demolished [by man], rather it sank in the ground through a miracle.

Similarly, since the verse, *Bnei Yisrael would thus move at Hashem's bidding, and at Hashem's bidding they would remain in one place* (*Bamidbar* 9:20), is enough to describe the basic facts, the reader might consider all the added details, such as: *And when the cloud remained over the Mishkan for a long time . . . and so it was when the cloud was a few days . . . Thus whether it was for a few days or a full year . . .* (*Bamidbar* 9:19-22) unnecessary. But these details were added to confirm the story, negating secular theories that the Jews had lost their way and did not know where to go, as Pharaoh said, *They are lost in the area and trapped in the desert* (*Shemos* 14:3). In fact, the Arabs call the desert, *bar altia*, "bewildering desert," imagining that the Jews had lost their way and did not know where to turn. The Torah therefore emphasizes that it was by G-d's command that the journeys followed an indirect route, that the Jews returned to the same places several times, and that they stayed for different periods of time in each station; staying in one place eighteen years, in another for one day, and in another place for just one night. All this happened at G-d's command. They had not lost their way, rather the route was determined by, *whenever the cloud rose up from the Tent, Bnei Yisrael would set out on the march* (*Bamidbar* 9:17). That is why the details are given . . .

Chapter Fifty-one

G-d's Supervision

This chapter is a conclusion, not containing anything that has not been discussed in previous chapters. It also describes how a person who has attained true knowledge of G-d worships Him, offering guidance on how to accomplish this level of worship which is the highest goal a person can attain. This chapter also describes how G-d watches over man in this world with Divine Providence until he passes on to the World-to-Come.

A Parable

I will begin this chapter with a parable. A king is in his palace; some of his subjects are in the city while others are abroad. Some of those inside the city have their backs toward the palace, facing the opposite direction, and others are trying to enter the palace seeking an audience with the king, but cannot see the palace. When they reach the palace, some people go around it as they search for the entrance gate; others pass through the gate and walk around the lobby; while a third group manages to enter the inner part of the palace, standing in the same room as the king. But even this third group does not speak to the king, because other things are required before they can hear the king's words or speak to him.

I will now explain the parable. The people who are abroad refer to people who have no religious belief, neither one based on their own reasoning nor one received by tradition. These are people like the Turks in the North, the Kushites in the South and similar folks in our region. They are on the level of primitive animals. In my opinion they are not human; they are lower than humans, but above monkeys, since they have the form and shape of men, and their intellect ranks above that of apes.

Those in the city standing with their backs toward the king's palace are thinkers who believe in a false ideology, either because they have drawn wrong conclusions from their own reasoning, or have adopted erroneous doctrines of others. Because of their false beliefs, the more these people think they are advancing, the more they are actually retreating from the royal palace. They are much worse than the first group, and under certain circumstances there may even be need to slay them, wiping out all traces of their ideology so others should not be led astray.

Those who want to enter the king's palace but cannot see it are the multitude of Jews who observe the mitzvos but are ignorant. Those who arrive at the palace but go around it are Jews who believe in the principles of the true faith which they received by way of tradition, engrossing themselves in the study of practical Halachah, but do not delve into the philosophical underpinnings of the Torah, nor do they try to prove the truth of the principles of faith.

Those who research the fundamentals of Judaism have entered the palace lobby where they reach different levels of understanding. Finally, those who have indeed proved everything that can be proved and have as true a knowledge of G-d as can be attained, have reached the goal and are inside the king's room. Dear son, as long as you study mathematics and logic, you are one of those who are outside, still searching for the entrance to the palace. Our Sages phrased it in a figurative sense, saying: "Ben Zoma is still outside." When you understand physics you have entered the courtyard and are on the way to the palace lobby. When you have graduated physics and mastered theology, you are in the king's palace having attained the level of the wise men that are at different stages of moral perfection.

Moshe Rabbeinu

Some individuals concentrate their thoughts solely on the spiritual realm, thinking of nothing except reaching closeness to G–d, learning about G-d's ways as much as the human mind can comprehend. These are the men in the parable who have entered the king's chamber—they are the prophets. One prophet directed all his thoughts on G-dliness, attaining the loftiest spiritual status. About him [the Torah] says: *[Moshe] remained there with Hashem forty days* (*Shemos* 34:28), asking questions and receiving answers, speaking to Him, and being addressed by Him in that holy place, deriving such elation over his attainment that he did not eat bread nor drink water for forty days. His intellect gained such strength that all coarse bodily functions were suspended, especially those connected with the sense of touch. Other prophets can merely see, some from close by and some from a distance, as [Yirmeyah] said, *Hashem appeared to me from afar* (*Yirmeyah* 31:3) . . .

A Plan for Perfection

All acts of worship, such as reading the Torah, praying, and the performance of other mitzvos, are intended to divert your thoughts from worldly concerns, helping you give your undivided attention to G-d. Therefore, if you pray by moving your lips as you face the wall, while thinking about your business; if you read the Torah with your tongue without thinking about what you are reading because your mind is on the construction of your house; if you perform the mitzvos only with your limbs, then you are like a person who is digging a hole in the ground or chopping wood in the forest robotically, without thinking of what he is doing or who told him to do it. Do not think you will attain perfection this way. On the contrary, you are like those about whom the prophet says, *You are close to their mouths but distant from their thoughts* (*Yirmeyah* 12:2).

Train yourself to obtain that great perfection by first turning your thoughts away from everything else while saying the *Shemah* or *Shemoneh esrei*. Moreover, don't be satisfied with intently reading only the first verse of *Shemah* or the first *berachah* of the *Shemoneh esrei*. When you have successfully done this for many years, begin focusing all your heart and thoughts on understanding the reading of the Torah. When you have successfully accomplished this, free your mind from any other thoughts when reading any books of the prophets, or when saying any *berachah;* concentrate exclusively on understanding what you are reading or saying. When you can perform these acts of worship properly, with your thoughts completely removed from worldly matters when doing them, then begin controlling your mind so it is not sidetracked by your personal needs or superfluous things. Think of worldly things while you eat, drink, bathe, talk with your wife and little children, or when chatting with other people. Those periods of time are frequent and long enough for you to manage your business, your household, and your health. But when you are engaged in Torah study and prayer, immerse yourself completely in what you are doing.

Use the precious moments when you are alone, awake in bed, to meditate on nothing but the rational worship of G-d, drawing close to Him and serving Him in the way that I have described to you—not in feigned exultation [expressed through outcry, bodily motions, and rolling the eyes toward heaven]. Through this program wise men can attain the highest perfection.

Moshe and the Patriarchs

If one acquires and rejoices in a true knowledge of G-d, so that even when he is interacting with people or taking care of his bodily needs, his mind and heart are constantly near G-d, then he has reached the stage which is described as, *I sleep, but my heart is awake; it is the voice of my beloved that knocks* (*Shir Hashirim* 5:2). Not all the prophets attained that status, but this was the level of Moshe Rabbeinu about whom it says, *Only Moshe shall then ap-*

proach Hashem, the others may not come close (*Shemos* 24:2), and, *You, however, must remain here with Me* (*Devarim* 5:28).

The Patriarchs, too, attained this degree of perfection, approaching G-d in such a way that His name became attached to them as it says, *The G-d of Avraham, the G-d of Yitzchak, and the G-d of Yaakov . . . This is My name forever* (*Shemos* 3:15). Their mind was completely filled with the knowledge of G-d; therefore He made an everlasting covenant with each of them, as it says, *I will remember My covenant with Yaakov . . .* (*Vayikra* 26:42). A number of verses teach us that the Patriarchs and Moshe had their mind filled exclusively with the knowledge and love of the name of G-d, and that in return, G-d's supervision closely watched over them and their descendants. Although we find them giving orders to people, engaged in earning money, and in managing their property, they only involved their bodily limbs with these things, but their heart and mind never moved away from G-d. These four men were granted the protection of G-d's supervision even in their business dealings, when feeding the flocks, working on the farms, or managing the houses, because their ultimate aim was to come as close as possible to G-d. Their primary goal in life was to create a nation that would know and serve G-d. And so it says, *I have given [Avraham] special attention so that he will command his children and his household after him, and they will keep Hashem's way, doing charity and justice* (*Bereishis* 18:19). The purpose of all their work was to spread the knowledge of G-d's Oneness throughout the world and to convince people to love Him; and because of that they succeeded in reaching that lofty spiritual stage where even their worldly activities were a perfect service of G-d. Someone like me should not imagine himself capable of reaching this degree of perfection. Rather, he can reach the level we mentioned previously, through the program we detailed above.

Let us pray to G-d that He remove from our path any obstruction that separates us from Him, even though most of the obstacles come from us, as we have explained based on the verse, *Your iniquities have separated between you and your G-d* (*Yeshayah* 59:2).

Why Bad Things Happen to Good People

I have a wonderful thought to dispel many doubts and reveal many spiritual mysteries. We have already stated in the chapters on G-d's supervision that His personal supervision watches over every thinking individual according to his intellect. Thus, His supervision rests at all times on those who never stop thinking of G–d. Those who are perfect in their knowledge of G-d, but at times turn their mind away from Him, will benefit from G-d's supervision while they meditate on Him, but G-d's supervision leaves them when their thoughts turn to other matters. His supervision does not abandon them like it abandons those who do not reflect on G-d at all; it is just less intense, because when a person with perfect knowledge of G-d is involved in worldly matters, his knowledge of G-d, though intact, is dormant, just like the abilities of a professional scribe when he is not writing. However, those who have no knowledge of G-d are like people who live in constant darkness and have never seen light. This is in line with our interpretation of the verse, *The wicked shall be silent in darkness* (1 *Shemuel* 2:9). Those constantly aware of the knowledge of G-d are, as it were, in bright sunshine, while the sun does not shine so brightly for those who have knowledge of G-d but are thinking of other things. It is a cloudy day for them; the sun does not shine on them because its light is blocked by the clouds [of other thoughts].

Therefore, it seems to me that if a prophet or a truly pious person is stricken with a mishap, it happens only while he is thinking of other things. [The severity of the adversity will] depend on the length of time and the subject matter of his thoughts.

This logic removes the difficulty that led philosophers to deny G-d's supervision over every single person and secularists to assert that man is like every other living being in this respect. They proved their theory by the fact that good men experienced great misfortunes. But we have explained this difficult question even according to the philosophers' own theory.

G-d's supervision is prepared for those who make an effort to obtain it, and He constantly watches over those who have obtained this heavenly favor. When a man's thoughts are undividedly focused on G-d, and he rejoices in that knowledge, it is impossible for any evil to befall him, for when he is with G-d, G-d is with him. But when he turns his thoughts away from G-d, G-d hides Himself from him, and he is exposed to any evil that might befall him, for it is only the spiritual connection with G-d that assures G-d's supervision and protection from evil accidents. While no evil will befall him during his times of imperfection, things can happen to him by chance. This thought is expressed in the Torah, *I will display My anger against them and abandon them. I will hide My face from them, and they will be [their enemies'] prey. Beset by many evils and troubles, they will say, "Isn't it because My G-d is no longer with me that these evils have befallen me."* (*Devarim* 31:17). It is clear that we ourselves cause G-d to hide His face, and the partition that separates us from G-d is of our own making. This thought is expressed in the words, *On that day I will utterly hide My face because of all the evil that they have done in turning to alien gods* (ibid. 31:18). Undoubtedly, what is true for the community is true for the individual as well.

Protection from Evil

A person is exposed to chance and vulnerable to destruction like cattle if he is separated from G-d; were G-d always on his mind, he would not be touched by any evil whatsoever. For G-d says, *Fear not, for I am with you. Be not dismayed, for I am your G-d* (*Yeshayah* 41:10), and, *When you pass through water I am with you, through rivers, they will not wash you away* (ibid. 43:2), meaning if you train yourself and obtain this higher wisdom, G-d's supervision will watch over you, protecting you from all evil, as it says, *Hashem is with me, I have no fear; how can man affect me?* (*Tehillim* 118:6), and, *Learn now to go with Him and you will stay whole* (*Iyov* 22:21), meaning, turn to Him, and you will be safe from all evil.

Consider the Song on Mishaps (*Tehillim* 91) and its description of the safeguard from all misfortune, whether collective or individual mishaps; from those caused by natural phenomena or from man. The verse says *He will deliver you from the ensnaring trap, from devastating pestilence. With His pinion He will cover you, and beneath His wings you will be protected. Shield and armor is His truth. You shall not fear the terror of night, nor the arrow that flies by day, nor the pestilence that walks in gloom, nor the destroyer who lays waste at noon* (*Tehillim* 91:3-5). The psalm describes how G-d protects us from distress caused by men, saying that if you face an army fighting with drawn swords, *A thousand will fall at your side and ten thousand at your right side, but to you they shall not come near. You will merely peer with your eyes, and you will see the retribution of the wicked* (ibid. v. 7,8). This is followed by the verse explaining the cause of this great protection, *For he has yearned for Me, and I will deliver him; I will elevate him, because he has known My name* (ibid. v.14). We have shown in previous chapters that "knowing My name" means having knowledge of G-d. The above verse should be understood in the following order: This man is protected because he has known Me and subsequently yearned passionately for Me. There is a difference between the term "to love" and the term to "yearn passionately." When a man's love is so intense that his thoughts are exclusively focused on his beloved, it is expressed by the words "yearn passionately."

Knowledge Increases with Age

A young man's vigor and vitality impede the development of moral principles, hampering the acquisition of pure thought. This is attained through an intense love of G-d which cannot be achieved while one's bodily fluids are seething. The weaker one's bodily forces become, and the more the fire of passion is doused, the more man's intellect increases, the sharper his perception becomes, and the happier he is with his knowledge. When a sage reaches old age and is near death, his knowledge greatly increases;

sensing an intense joy with that knowledge, his soul leaves the body in great delight.

The Sages had this feeling of exhilaration in mind when they said Moshe, Aharon, and Miriam, died "by a kiss," inferring this from the passage, *Moshe the servant of Hashem died there in the land of Moav by the mouth of Hashem* (*Devarim* 34:5). The same expression is used for Aharon, *Aharon haKohen went up Mount Hor . . . by the mouth of Hashem and died there* (*Bamidbar* 33:38). Our Sages said Miriam's death was likewise, but the phrase "by the mouth of Hashem" was not used since she was a woman and it was not suitable to describe her death with that terminology.

These three died delighting in knowing and loving G-d. The Sages followed the accepted poetic style of describing passionate love of G-d as "a kiss," as in, *Let Him kiss me with the kisses of His mouth* (*Shir Hashirim* 1:2). The Sages ascribe this death, which in fact is an escape from actual death, only to Moshe, Aharon, and Miriam. However, the other prophets and devout men who were on a lower spiritual level, non-the-less felt their knowledge of G-d become stronger at the time of death, as it says, *Your righteous deeds will precede you, and the glory of Hashem will gather you in* (*Yeshayah* 58:8). Since the obstacle [of their physical body] which at times stood in the way is now removed, these people's intellect remains permanently in this state of intense pleasure, which is not pleasure of the senses as we have previously explained.

Try to spend more and more time getting closer to G-d and less time on other things.

Chapter Fifty-two

Standing Before Hashem

One does not act in the privacy of his home the way he would behave in the presence of a great king. In the company of family and relatives he may talk and jests as he pleases, but not when he attends a royal cabinet meeting. Therefore, one who wishes to achieve human perfection, becoming a true man of G-d, must always be cognizant that the great king that accompanies him and is always joined to him is far greater than any human individual, greater even than David and Shelomoh. The king that clings to us and accompanies us is the intellect that motivates us and forms the link between G-d and man. Just as we perceive G-d through the light He sends down to us, as it says, *In Your light shall we see light* (*Tehillim* 36:9), so does G-d look at us by way of the same light He sends down to us. He is always with us, seeing us and watching us through this light, as it says, *Can a man hide in secret places that I shall not see him?* (*Yirmeyah* 23:24). Understand this well.

Modesty

When perfect men realize this, they attain humility, fear and reverence of G-d. They sense a feeling of genuine shame—not a contrived kind of shame—so they are as modest in their personal conduct, even when they are alone with their wives or in the bathroom, as they are when publicly interacting with other people. This is how our famous Sages conducted themselves with their wives. Indeed, the Sages said, "Who is modest? Whoever behaves at night as he behaves by day." They also warned against walking with a proud bearing, since, *The whole world is filled with His glory* (*Yeshayah* 6:3) and they wished to embed in our hearts the idea that we are always before G-d, walking in the presence of His glory. Indeed, the great Sages did not uncover their heads because the *Shechinah* hovers over us; for the same reason they spoke very little. In our Commentary on *Pirkei Avos* (1:17) we explained at length how we should restrict our speech, as it says, *For G-d is in heaven, and you are on earth; so let your words be few* (*Koheles* 5:1).

Love and Fear of G-d

This is the underlying theme of all mitzvos. By continuously performing all the particulars of the mitzvos, fearing G-d and being in awe of Him, some outstanding individuals may attain human perfection. Aware that G-d is with them, they will perform their duty. G-d states explicitly that the purpose of all mitzvos is to create fear of G-d and fervor for doing the mitzvos in man, as it says, *If you are not careful to keep all the words of this Torah, as written in this book, so as to fear this glorious, awesome name of Hashem your G-d* (*Devarim* 28:58). It clearly states that the sole purpose and aim of *all the words of this Torah* is to make us *fear this glorious, awesome name of Hashem*. That this aim is achieved through certain acts is derived from the wording of this verse, *If you are not careful to keep all the words of this Torah . . .*, which refers to observing the positive and the negative mitzvos.

The Torah teaches that belief in G-d's existence and His Oneness creates a love of G-d in us, as I have shown repeatedly. The Torah stresses the idea of love, as in, *Love Hashem your G-d with all your heart, with all your soul, and with all your resources* (*Devarim* 6:5). These two goals—love of G-d and fear of Him—are reached through different ways: Love of G-d is attained through the beliefs taught in the Torah, including the knowledge of the existence of G-d, while fear of G-d is achieved by performing the mitzvos, as I have explained. Understand this thesis.

Chapter Fifty-three

Chesed, Tzedakah and Mishpat

This chapter explains the meaning of three terms: *chesed* (loving-kindness), *mishpat* (judgment), and *tzedakah* (righteousness). We have explained in our commentary on *Pirkei Avos* (5:6), that in general, the term *chesed* denotes "excess." In most cases, however, it is applied to exceptional kindness. *Chesed* is practiced in two ways: firstly, by showing *chesed* to one who has earned no claim to kindness from us, and secondly by showing a greater measure of kindness to someone who has earned only a smaller measure of our kindness. In Tanach, the word *chesed* is generally used to show kindness to someone who has no right at all to claim it. Thus, the term *chesed* is used to express the goodness bestowed on us by G–d. For example, *Hashem's* chesed *will I proclaim* (*Yeshayah* 63:7). Therefore, creating the world is an act of *chesed* on the part of G-d, as it says, *For I said, "The world is built on* chesed*"* (*Tehillim* 89:34). When listing G-d attributes, the Torah says G-d is *Abundant in* chesed (*Shemos* 34:6).

The root of the word *tzedakah* is *tzedek*, "righteousness," which denotes the act of giving everyone his due and allotting to every being what he has earned. In Tanach, however, fulfilling one's duty toward others is not called *tzedakah;* when one gives a hired worker his wages or pays a debt, he is not lauded as giving *tzedakah.* Rather, *tzedakah* refers to fulfilling our moral obligations toward our fellow-men, for example, when we raise up those that are stumbling. Thus the Torah says about one who returns a pledge [to the poor debtor], *You will then have the merit of* tzedakah *before Hashem your G-d* (*Devarim* 24:11). When you follow the path of virtue, you act righteously toward your cognitive soul, paying it what it is entitled to be paid. Because every moral virtue is called *tzedakah*, the Torah applies this term to the virtue of faith in G-d, as it says, *[Avraham] believed in Hashem, and He counted it as tzedakah* (*Bereishis* 15:6), and, *It will be considered tzedakah if we safeguard and keep this entire mandate* (*Devarim* 6:25).

The word *mishpat* (judgment) means deciding the verdict of one who is judged, whether to his benefit or detriment.

To summarize: The word *chesed* denotes unconditional kindness; *tzedakah* refers to every good deed you do as a moral obligation and as a means of perfecting your soul, while *mishpat* sometimes leads [the defendant] to liability and sometimes to benefit.

Divine Attributes

We have already said that the Divine attributes in Tanach are descriptions of G-d's actions; thus He is called *chasid* (kind), because He created the universe; *tzaddik* (righteous) for His mercy towards the weak and for providing every living being according to its needs; *shofeit* (judge) because of the great munificence and calamities that occur in the world, decreed by G-d's justice based on His wisdom. These three attributes are found in the *Chumash* in the following passages: *Shall the whole world's Judge* [shofeit] *not act justly?* (*Bereishis* 18:25); *Righteous* (tzaddik) *and upright is He* (*Devarim* 32:4); *Abundant in loving kindness* (chesed).

These explanations are a preface for the next chapter.

Chapter Fifty-four

Attaining Perfection

The Hebrew word *chochmah* (wisdom) is used for four different concepts:

Chochmah means grasping the truth which leads to knowledge of G-d, as it says, [*As for*] chochmah: *Where can it be found?* (*Iyov* 28:12), and, *If you seek* [chochmah] *as [if it were] silver* (*Mishlei* 2:4). The word occurs frequently in this sense.

The word *chochmah* also denotes craftsmanship, as in, *And every wise-hearted* [chacham leiv] *among you shall come forth and make all that Hashem has ordered* (*Shemos* 35:10), and, *All the wise-hearted* [chochmas leiv] *women did spin* (ibid. 35:25).

It is also used to describe acquiring moral character traits, as in, *To make his elders wise* (*Tehillim* 105:22), and, *In the aged is* chochmah (*Iyov* 12:12), for moral qualities are formed, for the most part, in old age.

Finally, the word *chochmah* denotes aptitude for scheming and conniving, as in, *Come on, we must deal wisely* [nis'chakemah] *with them* (*Shemos* 1:10). The word is used in the same sense in the following verse, *[Yoav] brought a wise woman from there* (2 *Shemuel* 14:2), meaning that she had a talent for ploys and deception. In this sense it says, *They are wise at doing evil* (*Yirmeyah* 4:22).

Possibly, the word *chochmah* always means cunning and planning. At times one may plan to acquire scholarly perfection or moral virtues, at other times he wishes to acquire skill in craftsmanship, and at still other times he will use his cunning for deception to achieve evil and wickedness.

Thus the term *chacham* can be applied to one who is very intelligent, one with moral virtue, one skilled in a craft, and even to a devious and evil person.

In light of this explanation, a person who has a true knowledge of the Torah is called *chacham* for two reasons: because the Torah fills him with intellectual prowess and because it bolsters his moral fiber.

Torah and Philosophy

Since the laws of the Torah are taught by way of tradition, rather than intellectual theorizing, the books of the Prophets and the sayings of our Sages refer to the study of the Torah as separate from the *chochmah* of philosophy. The wisdom of philosophy which proves intellectually what the Torah teaches us by way of tradition is what they refer to as *chochma*. All the verses extolling wisdom and bemoaning the fact that only few people possess it, refer to the wisdom of abstract rational thought, which confirms the truth of the Torah. And so it says, *Not many are wise* (*Iyov* 32:9), and, [*As for*] chochmah*: Where can it be found?* (ibid. 28:12). There are many other passages to that effect.

Many passages in the sayings of our Sages make a distinction between knowledge of the Torah and the wisdom of philosophy. They say about Moshe Rabbeinu that he was "Father [i.e., leader] in Torah, father in *chochmah*, and father in prophecy." Although it says about Shelomoh, *He was wiser than all men* (1 *Melachim* 5:11), our Sages added, "but not greater than Moshe." The phrase "wiser than all men" must therefore be interpreted to mean, "wiser than all men of his generation." For this reason only *Heiman, Chalcol, and Darda*, *sons of Machal* (1 *Melachim* 5:11), the famous wise men of his time are mentioned.

Account Before the Heavenly Tribunal

Our Sages tell us that [after his demise] a person must render an account [before the Heavenly Tribunal], of how much Torah he learned, about the wisdom he has acquired, and about how well he understands the legal issues of the Torah and what he is required to do. These questions are listed in the proper order. One must first learn the Torah principles as taught by tradition, then one must learn how to prove them intellectually, and finally, he must carefully do the mitzvos to improve his way of life. Our Sages expressed the idea this way: When a man comes before judgment [in the World to Come] he is asked: "Did you fix times for learning Torah? Did you delve into the intricacies of wisdom? Have you inferred one concept from another concept?" This proves that our Sages delineated between the knowledge of Torah as one kind of calling and the acquisition of *chochmah* as a different pursuit and as a means of proving the truth of the Torah through rational thought.

Four Types of Perfection

Both the early and contemporary philosophers have explained that man can attain four kinds of perfection. The first and lowest standard of perfection, which common people crave, is the perfection of wealth, including money, clothing, furniture, slaves, land, and the like. Even a great king aspires to this kind of perfection. But there is no actual connection between wealth and an owner of wealth. The enjoyment he derives from his possessions, when boasting, "This is my house, my slave, my money, my army," is purely imaginary. These things are not part of him and each of these possessions exists independent of him. Therefore, when this relationship comes to an end, the greatest king will find himself no different than the lowliest pauper, despite the fact that no change took place in the things he once owned. The philosophers explain that a person who strives with all his might for this type of perfection is chasing an imaginary and fleeting mirage. Even if he retains his riches throughout his life, he will not thereby achieve genuine inner perfection.

The second [perfection], which is perfect health and strong and well-proportioned limbs has a greater connection to a person's individuality than the first, but it is also not ideal, for physical perfection is not a uniquely human characteristic, but rather something man has in common with the lowliest forms of life. Even the strongest man is no match for a strong mule, much less for a lion or an elephant. At best he is able to carry a heavy load or crack a thick bone or do other such things in which there is no great benefit for the body. Surely this kind of perfection has no benefit for the soul.

The third kind of perfection relates more closely to a person's inner self than the second kind. It is the perfection of moral and ethical qualities by which a person reaches the highest degree of virtue and rectitude. Most mitzvos are aimed at helping man reach this perfection. But even this kind of perfection is only a stepping stone toward a higher form of perfection; it is not the ultimate objective in and of itself. For all the rules of ethics and morality apply to the relationship between man and his neighbor. You might say that the perfection of moral traits is intended for the benefit of mankind. Were a person to live in total seclusion, isolated from any other person, all his moral virtues would be useless, giving him no perfection at all. He only needs them and they only become useful when he comes into contact with others.

The fourth kind of perfection, which is the true perfection of man, is the attainment of intellectual mastery, comprehending the essence of G-d through contemplation. This is the ultimate goal of human thought which grants true perfection to a person—to his internal self—giving [his soul] immortality. This is what makes him a human being.

The other three perfections relate to others, not to one's self, even though, on the surface, they seem to involve both one's self and others. But the fourth kind of perfection *is yours alone, and no one else shares it with you* (*Mishlei* 5:17). Therefore, strive to attain this fourth perfection that is yours alone; don't weary yourself working for others while forgetting your own soul which is becoming tarnished from your bodily impulse. The poetic verses alluding to this theme says, *My mother's children quarreled with me. They made me guard the vineyards, my own vineyard I did not guard*

(*Shir Hashirim* 1:6). The following passage also refers to this theme, *Lest you give your glory to others, and your [remaining] years to the cruel one*[34] (*Mishlei* 5:9).

Confirmed by the Prophets and Sages

The prophets describe these concepts as the philosophers, stating clearly that the perfection of wealth, good health, or virtuous traits is nothing to be proud of or desired. They conclude that the only perfection one should be proud of and desire is the knowledge of G-d, for this is true enlightenment.

Speaking of these four kinds of perfections, Yirmeyah says, *Thus said Hashem: Let not the wise man glorify himself with his wisdom, and let not the strong man glorify himself with his strength, and let not the rich man glorify himself with his wealth. For only with this may one glorify himself—contemplating and knowing Me, [for I am Hashem who does kindness, justice, and righteousness on the earth, for in these things is My delight, says G-d]* (*Yirmeyah* 9:22,23).

Notice how the prophet arranged [the perfections in ascending order as they are regarded by the masses]. In the eyes of the masses the greatest perfection is, *the rich man with his wealth.* The level below that is, *the strong man with his strength,* and the level below that is, *the wise man with his wisdom*, meaning, a person of moral character, for a wise man is also regarded with respect by the multitudes who Yirmeyah is addressing. This is why the three kinds of perfection are arranged in this order.

Our Sages derived from this verse that the word *chochmah* means acquiring knowledge of G-d, that all other kinds of perfection which people aspire to are not perfect, and that performing mitzvos, praying, and moral conduct are not the ultimate goal of man's existence. They are only the means toward reaching the goal [of knowledge of G-d].

Thus, the Sages in *Bereishis Rabbah* say: *And all desires cannot*

34 The master of Gehinnom who exacts punishment from sinners (Rashi).

compare to [wisdom] (*Mishlei* 8:11). Another verse says, *all your desires cannot compare to [wisdom]* (ibid. 3:15). The Sages explain that] *all desires* refer to mitzvos and good deeds, whereas *your desires* refer to precious stones and pearls. Both—*all desires* and *your desires*—cannot compare to wisdom, *For only with this may one glorify himself—contemplating and knowing Me.* Consider how concise this saying is, and how perfect is [Shelomoh] the one who said it, omitting nothing in this verse of all that we explained at length.

Emulating G-d's Attributes

Since we mentioned this verse and its lofty underlying idea as well as the comments of the Sages on it, we will explain the last segment of this verse. The prophet is not satisfied with explaining that the knowledge of G-d is the highest kind of perfection, for if this were all he had in mind, he would have said, *For only with this may one glorify himself—contemplating and knowing Me*—Or he might have said, "contemplating and knowing Me, that I am One," or, "that I do not have any likeness," or, "that there is none like Me," or words to that effect. But the prophet [adds, *for I am Hashem who does kindness, justice, and righteousness on the earth,*] saying that man can glory only in the knowledge of G-d combined with the knowledge of His ways and His attributes, meaning, His deeds, as we have explained in our commentary on the verse, *Allow me to know Your ways* (*Shemos* 33:13). Thus we are told in this verse that G-d's deeds which should be known and emulated are: *chesed* (kindness), *mishpat,* (justice), and, *tzedakah,* (righteousness).

G-d's Supervision Extends to Heaven and Earth

The prophet then adds a very important phrase: *in the land.* These words teach a pivotal principle of the Torah, repudiating the brazen folks who maintain that G-d's Providence does not extend to the area below the orbit of the moon, and that the earth and its inhabitants are left to fend for themselves. They say, *Hashem has forsaken the earth* (*Yechezkel* 8:12). In rebuttal, [Moshe,] the master of all wise men, proclaims, *The whole world belongs to Hashem* (*Shemos* 9:29), meaning G-d's supervision extends to the concerns of the earth as it extends to the concerns of heaven. This is [how Yirmeyah] expresses this idea, *For I am Hashem who does kindness, justice, and righteousness on the earth* (*Yirmeyah* 9:23), concluding, *for in these things is My delight, says G-d.* The prophet means it is G-d's will that through us, kindness, justice, and righteousness should prevail on earth. We explained in our commentary of the Thirteen Divine attributes that G-d wants us to emulate and live by these character traits. Thus, the ideal which [the prophet] speaks of in this verse is acquiring the knowledge of G-d to the best of one's ability, and understanding how G-d supervises the activities and conduct of His creatures. This is a perfection in which a person may truly take pride. Having acquired this knowledge, he will always seek to imitate G-d's ways, leading his life with kindness, justice, and righteousness.

Conclusion

I thought this subject would be suitable for this book and beneficial to a person like you. I hope that after earnest reflection, you will, with G-d's help, understand all the points I have discussed in it. May He grant us and all Yisrael that which He has promised us, *Then the eyes of the blind will be opened, and the ears of the deaf will be unstopped* (*Yeshayah* 35:5). *The people that walked in darkness have seen a great light. Those who dwelled in the land of the shadow of death, light has shone on them* (ibid. 9:1). **Amen**

G-d is very near to all who call on Him,
if they call on Him in truth, without pause.
He is found by whoever intently seeks Him,
if he walks toward Him without swerving.

GLOSSARY

AZAZEL - The goat sent to the desert on Yom Kippur for atonement
BAMIDBAR - The Book of Numbers
BEIS HAMIDRASH - Torah study hall
BEIS HAMIKDASH - Holy Temple
BEREISHIS - The Book of Genesis
BNEI YISRAEL - Children of Israel
CHUKIM - Decrees
DEVARIM - The Book of Deuteronomy
EIGEL HAZAHAV - The Golden Calf
ERETZ YISRAEL - The Land of Israel
GEMARA - Talmud
HALACHAH pl. *HALACHOS* - Law
HASHEM - God
KOHEN GADOL - High Priest
KOHEN pl. *KOHANIM* - Priests, descendants of Aaron
KORBAN pl. *KORBANOS* - Sacrifice
MIDRASH – Homiletic Discourse
MIKVEH - Ritual immersion pool
MILAH - Circumcision
MISHNAH pl. *MISHNAYOS* - Compilation of the oral tradition; it also refers to one paragraph of this compilation
MITZVAH pl. *MITZVOS* - Commandment
MOREH NEVUCHIM - Guide for the Perplexed
MOSHE RABBEINU - Moses our Teacher
NAZIR - Nazirite, one who makes a vow to abstain from wine and from contact with the dead
RAMBAM - Maimonides
RAMBAN - Nachmanides
ROSH CHODESH - The first day of the Hebrew month, which is a minor holiday
SANHEDRIN - Jewish High Court
SEFER - Book or scroll

SHABBOS - The day of rest, Saturday
SHAVUOS - Festival of Weeks
SHECHINAH - Divine Presence
SHECHITAH - Ritual slaughter
SHEMAH - The portion of the Torah containing the declaration of Hashem's unity that we say morning and evening
SHEMINI ATZERES - The last day of the Succos Festival
SHEMONEH ESREI - The eighteen beracha prayer that we say thrice each day
SHEMOS - The Book of Exodus
SHIR HASHIRIM - Song of Songs
SHMITTAH - The sabbatical year when work in the field is prohibited
SHOFAR - Ram's horn blown on Rosh Hashana
SOTAH – A suspected adultress
SUKKAH - Hut used on Sukkos
TAHARAH - Ritual purity
TAMEI - Ritually impure
TANACH - Scriptures
TEFILLIN - Phylacteries
TEHILLIM - Psalms
TESHUVAH - Repentance
TUMAH - Ritual impurity
TZEDAKAH - Charity
TZITZIS - Fringes worn on a four cornered garment
VAYIKRA - The Book of Leviticus
YAAKOV - Jacob
YAMIM TOVIM - Holidays
YEHOSHUA - Joshua
YERUSHALAYIM - Jerusalem
YESHAYAH - Isaiah
YETZER HARA - Evil inclination
YISRAEL - Israel
YITZCHOCK - Isaac